Factoring:
Sell Your Invoices Today,
Get Cash Tomorrow

How to Obtain Unlimited Funds
Without a Loan

Jeff Callender

DASH POINT PUBLISHING

Federal Way, Washington

Factoring: Sell Your Invoices Today, Get Cash Tomorrow

How to Get Unlimited Funds Without a Loan

by Jeff Callender

Published by:
Dash Point Publishing, Inc.
P.O. Box 25591
Federal Way, WA 98093-2591 U.S.A.

Website: www.DashPointPublishing.com

Library of Congress Control Number: 2012943559
ISBN: 978-1-938837-05-0 (Paperback)
ISBN: 978-1-938837-17-3 (PDF)
ISBN: 978-1-938837-23-4 (Kindle)
ISBN: 978-1-938837-11-1 (ePub)

Printed in the United States of America.

Dedication

To

Mike Barrette

My Lifelong Friend

Contents

Preface

What do business owners who factor say about the service? On the following pages are comments taken from several factors' web sites.

Business Owners' Comments about Factoring

"It's wonderful to make deposits weekly to meet my overhead. Bills don't stop coming in and now I can pay them stress-free. Factoring is a very cost-effective way of running my business and eliminates a load of worry."

"For those who wait (and wait) for state and federal checks on appointed work, use this service to get paid quickly."

"Factoring gives us the working capital we need without having to wait 30 or more days to get paid. We have cash available now any time we have an order so we're able to do our purchasing and fill our customers' orders right away. This has helped us a lot."

"Our decision to factor has made it possible for our business to flourish. Cash flow stress has been eliminated. We have a working arrangement that is a simple formula for success for all parties, i.e. manufacturer, supplier, retail stores and factor."

"We have always felt that success comes with knowing what you do best and doing it, and delegating other aspects that you are not as experienced in to others. Therefore we spend our time and resources producing and selling our products and turn over the 'financing of our sales' to our factor. Their experience in credit and collections has enabled us to grow without the usual stress of unpredictable cash flow. Our association is not just the best financial arrangement that we could make, but one of teamwork."

"Prior to factoring, our cash flow was badly strapped due to growth of receivables and new accounts. Because of factoring, we have been able to take on more major business accounts. The obvious benefit is that it has freed our cash and enabled us to continue our growth. We feel it has been an excellent decision."

"Our invoices are sent on a weekly basis and the virtually seamless operation of funding for our invoices provides us the timely deposit of funds into our bank account, usually the same day of funding if a bank wire is used. My receivables are in remarkably better shape since enlisting the invoice management of my factor."

"Factoring has allowed me to free up more time to concentrate on my business needs rather than to have to chase down income."

"Our company has been able to keep our head above water by having funds available every week instead of waiting for months for capital to come in."

"Our factor has become a true partner in providing the service we need. Without their help it would have been impossible for us to achieve the level of business that we are at now."

"I have noticed that my collections are coming in quicker now than ever before."

"Factoring our invoices has freed up our cash and allowed us to begin expansion programs."

"Without our factoring company, we would be struggling with our business. Instead we are expanding and growing rapidly. We look forward to growing aggressively knowing that we have the support of our factor."

"We were in the 'red' until our factor came to our rescue. We are a small company that just could not get enough cash flow to expand. Our accounts receivable were stacking up, and having to wait 30 to 45 days to get paid was putting us at a standstill. The thought of getting a small business loan with a high interest rate just made the future look even dimmer. However, when we were told about our factor and what they have done for other businesses, we thought we would give them a try. That was the best move we have made! Now we are back on track and are planning to expand within the next few months. Thank you for giving us the security of a timely paycheck."

"With the kind of work I do it is like that old saying 'hurry up and wait,' work now pay later, sometimes much later. If it were not for factoring, at this point I would probably not have a business. Factoring really takes the pressure off!"

"Factoring has enabled our company to have a positive cash flow each week. Also factoring has enhanced our ability to save 2% off our suppliers' accounts each month – enhancing our company to be able to hire new employees and expand. We appreciate the service and are looking forward to a long future together."

"As a new company we have taken advantage of factoring to allow us to function with more financial freedom than we could otherwise. Being able to receive a large portion of our invoices as they are sent out gives us the ability to use our own capital instead of having to get a small business loan."

"Factoring has provided a means to succeed. This method provides convenience and stability that I pass on to my customers. My company would not exist without factoring."

"We have a small printing company and have been doing our own bookkeeping and holding our accounts receivable for twenty-four years. At times during the month we might have to pay a $5500 paper bill and make payroll and we would go to our post office box and find maybe $600 in checks from clients, and fall short on our promises. Factoring is the best move we've ever made in our business. It has helped us effectively maximize our cash flow and keep on track with our payables. It's also given us accurate reports and more time to spend on production and new sales. We remain in control with the collection process with our customers. It's also allowed us to do more business with our customers. Overall it gives the business owner more free time to do what only they can do and that's to build their business with the extra time gained. And most importantly, one of the best features is the feeling of peace of mind."

"Factoring has truly made a difference in our company. After three years of trying to get a loan at our bank, we finally were able to qualify for a large one due to the fact that through factoring we could show and guarantee that the money would always be coming in at a specific time and approximately the same amount every month. It has also helped our management and control over all aspects of the business."

"As a contractor for large corporations, I'm not always paid in a timely manner. With factoring, I'm able to receive an immediate payment, have my accounts receivable taken care of, and receive up to date information of my factoring account."

"As a small business owner with visions to grow, financial stability and cash are necessities. With factoring we have managed to grow and prosper. Factoring has given us the means to achieve our goals and has made it possible for our company to triple our gross receipts in just a year's time. This program works and it could work for you."

I begin this book with the comments of business owners who are likely to be much like you: hard-working, running a successful (or potentially successful) business, knowing their companies *could* flourish. Yet each of these owners has run into a familiar but serious problem: their cash flow was "up a creek."

Notice two consistent themes in these comments. Factoring has provided:

1) **Financial benefits** for the companies. They have increased financial stability; cash to meet payroll, pay bills, fund growth, accept new business, and hire staff; and more time to devote to profitable activities.

2) **Emotional benefits** for the business owners. They have less stress and worry; newly found peace of mind, security, and convenience; and are able to maintain control of their company.

What's more, a helpful new member has been added to the firm's team: the factor himself.

These entrepreneurs' statements are just a small sliver of what many have experienced for years: factoring helps their companies enormously. By utilizing the information in this book and making use of the tools presented, you may find factoring to be exactly the instrument your business needs to solve your cash flow needs.

If you, the business owner, and/or your company can benefit from any or all of the advantages factoring provides, you will find the information in this book exceptionally valuable.

Jeff Callender

Part 1

Discovery

Factoring: Sell Your Invoices Today, Get Cash Tomorrow

1
Introduction

A True Story

Jerry was born with an entrepreneurial spirit. After working years in various jobs for other people, he wanted nothing more than to be his own boss. Finally he decided to strike out on his own and begin his own business.

After months of preparation he opened his doors as the proud owner of a small sign shop. Serving the local market, his business created banners, A-frame signs, window lettering, vehicle graphics, and the typical products small vinyl shops provide.

After the initial startup costs for his storefront, rent, equipment, and materials, he had enough capital to hire an employee and get under way. Like most startups, the first few months were slow as expected but business improved somewhat each month. He wasn't setting the world on fire, but he was optimistic.

He had enough working capital to operate for what turned out to be about six months. When he began, Jerry thought this would be enough to get under way until the store became profitable. He had his materials, a good location, and everything needed to begin selling his products. He was conscientious and hard-working, put in many long hours, and enjoyed being his own boss.

With his good location and modest marketing efforts, customers found their way into Jerry's shop and placed their orders. Smaller purchases were paid up front, while larger ones required half down at the time of the sale and the balance upon completion. Most customers paid with a credit card and some paid in cash.

During the early months Jerry's sales were not quite what he had hoped. He realized his sales needed to increase, and this could be done by increasing the number of his typical small customers, or gaining a few customers who would place consistent, large orders.

One day a woman walked into his shop and inquired about some banners she needed. Like most new customers, she asked about the design, size, colors, material, delivery time, and price. After learning about Jerry's products and prices she seemed clearly interested in placing an order. Most new customers who asked the same questions she asked usually just wanted one or two banners. He expected this to be a fairly routine order. But then she dropped a bombshell.

This woman – dressed more professionally than most of his customers, Jerry thought when she first walked in – was the regional vice president of a well known self-storage company. This company had a substantial number of franchises in the area. Not only did she need a large number of banners which would be used at all the stores in the region, she needed them relatively quickly. And because of the number of banners she wanted, she required a significant discount from his regular price. Would he be able to deliver? If her company was happy with this order, there would be many future orders this size and larger. Oh, and by the way...her company would require 45 day payment terms with no down payment.

As any business owner will appreciate, her required terms posed a dilemma for Jerry. This was exactly the kind of new customer he needed, ordering in large volume with a steady and dependable flow. He wanted nothing more than to make not only this big sale, but the ones that would follow. This customer could mean steady and sorely-needed income for his young company, and she could help establish his business further with referrals from the circle of contacts she and her associates could provide.

However, waiting 45 days to receive payment created two immediate problems for Jerry:

1. He would need to order a significant amount of new materials to make this many banners...and his suppliers would demand payment from him before he would be paid by this new customer.

2. He would need to hire extra help to get the banners made in time. This would temporarily swell his payroll and require even more cash out of pocket before he would be paid.

What should Jerry do? Should he turn down this order because he didn't have the cash needed to meet the customer's requirements? Or should he accept the order and then scramble like mad trying to come up with the cash needed to fill the order? What would happen to his business if he accepted the order but then couldn't deliver because of inadequate capital?

Many business owners face Jerry's dilemma on a regular basis. They may also be small shop owners, or lead much larger corporations dealing with millions of dollars of annual sales. However the problem presents itself, the dilemma is the same: "How can I grow my company – or simply keep it running – when I don't have enough cash?"

Regardless of the size of your business or your industry, this book will address a well-established but often unknown solution to the problem of slow cash flow. While this answer will not be suitable or available for every single business, it does work for a great many. Surprisingly, many business owners have never even heard of it, despite the fact that this type of financing has been around for centuries.

The Need for Cash

If you are thinking about starting a business or are already the owner of one, chances are high that sooner or later you will find yourself in Jerry's position of needing more money than you have on hand. Maybe you're just starting from scratch and have little more than a great idea or business plan, or maybe you've been in business for some time and have a long list of customers. In either case, inadequate cash on hand is a very common problem. It can happen for many more reasons than just wanting to fill a big order, as Jerry did.

Even if a business is started with adequate capitalization, it can burn through early reserves at a surprising rate. Whether sales are slow or exceeding projections, new or young companies usually require further capital to continue. This is true whether a company is struggling or successful; in fact successful businesses often need more cash. Their very success depends on the availability of cash to keep up with orders, meet payroll, pay bills and taxes, and meet all the financial obligations a business owner knows all too well.

Often a small business will get under way with funds the owner has saved, inherited, obtained from the sale of property or assets, borrowed from friends and relatives, charged to credit cards, and otherwise pulled together. These may be enough to enable the enthusiastic entrepreneur to open the doors for business, obtain the first few months' orders, and realize the business can succeed. Yet many business owners run into a brick wall, despite (or because of) their success. Often this happens anywhere from two months to five years after they begin. It also happens to companies who have been in business for as many as fifteen or twenty years. What happens? Their cash on hand is not adequate to meet their expenses. In short, they have a cash flow problem.

Not enough cash on hand usually results from any or all of the following reasons.

1. Expenses are higher than expected.
2. Income is less than expected.
3. Receiving customer payments takes longer than the expenses required to fill orders.

When customers pay a business with cash or a credit card and that business runs short of cash, the cash flow problem usually can be traced to number 1 and/or number 2 above. When this is the case, the business owner needs to make adjustments to trim expenses and/or increase sales. This is commonly the case when a business' customers are consumers.

Companies whose customers are other businesses or government entities can easily experience all three of the above problems. Like businesses selling to consumers, business-to-business and business-to-government companies need to make adjustments to address numbers 1 and 2. Yet as we saw in Jerry's case, selling to companies or government agencies often necessitates extending terms to these customers in order to make the sale. Terms are often 30 or 45 days, but can be as much as 60 or 90 days for very large corporations. If a company cannot or will not extend the required terms, they lose a lot of potential business to competitors who will. This was Jerry's dilemma.

He needed some quick cash to pay his costs for this order, but where could he find it? His own funds were exhausted and his credit cards maxed out. He couldn't go to his relatives and friends again, and his business was much too young and not financially strong enough to qualify for a bank loan or line of credit.

Even if he could get an SBA loan he couldn't wait that long to fill this order. Besides, he'd burn through the small amount it would provide and he'd need more cash later anyway. Venture capital was an unlikely long shot, would take way too long, and wasn't suited to his industry. Even if it was, such funding would demand equity in his company and possibly even take over control. Obviously, Jerry was between a rock and a hard place. So what did he do?

He accepted the order and was able to obtain more than enough cash to purchase his materials and meet his payroll for this order. The cash was available, yet locked in his company through funds the order itself would provide later. Still, Jerry was able to tap into that cash long before the customer ever paid a dime. How?

Fortunately, he knew of an alternative form of financing few business owners understand and many are not even aware exists. Jerry knew a funding company that was eager to buy the invoice created for this order. With this knowledge he was able to **unlock the cash in his company** by selling his invoice for immediate cash.

How did he do this? Quite simply:

1. He accepted the order.
2. He arranged for the funding company to purchase his receivable.
3. He ordered his materials and hired enough help to make the product.
4. He delivered the product and created the invoice.
5. He sold the invoice and immediately was paid a large percent of the invoice's face value.

With plenty of cash now in hand, Jerry paid his suppliers, met payroll, and still had enough funds to meet other business obligations and accept more orders. What's more, the next time the self-storage company returned with another order for new banners, he welcomed their business and again *factored* (sold) the new invoice for immediate cash. Because his account was established, he didn't need to reapply as he would have for another SBA or bank loan. All he needed was another invoice to this creditworthy customer, and he received his cash in about one day's time...rather than waiting weeks or months.

In fact, because Jerry could provide 30 day terms to other large customers, more and bigger orders started to come in...which he factored as well. Thus his business expanded beyond small consumer orders (which he continued to receive) and he had plenty of cash to accept any orders that came his way.

Jerry had learned – and utilized – the secret of *unlocking the cash* in his company. What's more, this secret would provide *unlimited funds* for his business while generating *no debt* to repay, as a loan would. And even better, obtaining this cash would occur much faster than any loan process he would ever undergo. Access to this cash would not depend on his having good credit, he could qualify despite the short time he had been in business, and more cash could be obtained easily any time in the future. All he'd need would be more orders like this one from customers like this nicely dressed woman who walked into his shop.

Jerry smiled self-confidently as these thoughts ran through his mind. Business was looking up.

2
What Is Factoring?

The Definition of Factoring

By definition, factoring is the purchase of accounts receivable at a discount. That is, a factor is a person or business that pays immediate cash (somewhat less than the invoices' face value) for business receivables. As we have seen, an unpaid invoice that will be paid by a financially strong company has value. Factors pay cash for the right to receive the future payments on clients' invoices to their customers.

Factoring is not a loan with interest due, but the sale of an asset for which a discount is paid. That distinction is important as we'll see in a minute.

How much does factoring cost and how does it work? The amount a factor advances and the cost in discounts paid by a factoring client can vary widely and depend on

1. the company's industry
2. the creditworthiness of the customers
3. how long the customers take to pay
4. the dollar volume of the factored invoices.

However, for the sake of simplicity we'll use the following example to illustrate a typical and modest transaction. Suppose a factor purchases a $1,000 invoice and gives an 80% advance and charges 5% of the face value of the invoice, assuming payment is received in 30 days. (Any of these numbers might be higher or lower.)

After providing the advance ($800 the client now uses for any business need at hand) and waiting 30 days, the factor receives payment for the full $1,000 from the customer. When this payment arrives, the factor repays himself the $800 advanced, keeps 5% or $50 as a discount, and rebates the client the remaining 15%, or $150. Thus the client has paid $50 to receive $950, $800 of which he received immediately.

How Factoring Improves Cash Flow

When Jerry started factoring, he had just one customer whose invoice he needed to sell. The rest of his customers paid with cash or credit cards and there was no need to factor them. He already had received the cash needed to fill their orders.

The principle behind accepting credit cards is essentially the same as factoring. By paying a discount to the credit card company, Jerry receives cash within a few days and his customers send payment to the credit card company. By factoring his invoices, he is doing the very same thing: he pays the factoring company a discount to receive immediate cash, and his customers pay the factor.

Many businesses have many customers who wait weeks or even months to pay their bills. Not surprisingly, this delay frequently results in a cash flow problem for the vendors to whom they owe money. By selling to a factor multiple invoices to multiple customers, a company receives a quick and regular infusion of needed capital to run its operation. The owner's stress caused by waiting for payment is eliminated and cash flow becomes dependable. This enables expansion to move forward as new markets open up, needed staff is hired, and/or needed equipment is added.

What's more, cash from factored receivables allows the business owner to meet other regular business needs such as:

- meeting payroll
- paying taxes
- purchasing supplies
- funding marketing efforts
- taking advantage of discounts for paying with cash.

Factoring receivables for these common business needs is a dependable means of providing capital for a company when traditional funds are unavailable.

Service businesses with few products but heavy payroll responsibilities such as staffing agencies, guard services, cleaning companies, and the like can take on new business knowing their payroll will be met easily with factoring advances. Likewise, manufacturing and product-intensive companies such as Jerry's can have ready cash to replenish inventory and create more products, without having to wait for earlier sales to be paid. In both cases these businesses can grow and the owner is relieved from worrying about how to pay the bills necessary to the company's survival.

A simple way to determine how factoring can improve *your* company's cash flow is to answer this question: "If my company had all the cash on hand it needed, what would I do with that cash?" Chances are good you would answer, "Some or all of the above" – meet payroll, purchase materials, pay bills, meet tax obligations, fund marketing campaigns, take advantage of cash discounts, and so on.

In whatever way you imagine using the cash, if you find yourself smiling and feel a degree of stress lifting from your shoulders at the thought of these concerns going away, then your cash flow is probably not as good as you would like. If you have receivables to creditworthy business or government customers, factoring can very likely be the answer you've been looking for.

The Difference Factoring Makes

How can you calculate whether factoring will improve your company's bottom line? Below is a simplified Income Statement of a manufacturing company, though as you know factoring can benefit numerous other types of businesses. Let's look closely at this statement, learn how to "read" the information, and then see how to apply this to your situation.

	Before Factoring
Gross Revenues	100,000
Cost of Goods Sold	60,000
Gross Profits	40,000
Less:	
Variable Expenses	15,000
Fixed Expenses	20,000
Overhead	35,000
Cost of Factoring	0
Total Expenses	35,000
Net Profit	5,000

As you can see, this company starts with $100,000 worth of invoices. The number of zeros isn't an issue, so if your company is larger or smaller, just add or delete a zero or two. However the larger your volume, the lower your factoring discount will be. Companies with smaller volume will have somewhat higher factoring costs.

This company's Cost of Goods Sold is 60% of its Gross Revenues, leaving 40% in Gross Profits. Its Variable Expenses are $15,000 and Fixed Expenses (which will be constant) are $20,000, resulting in Overhead costs of $35,000. This leaves a Net Profit of $5,000.

Now let's suppose the company begins factoring a large portion of its receivables, and in so doing its volume actually doubles. This increase could come from the ability to accept new or more customers, increasing sales staff, purchasing additional equipment to boost production, shifting staff from servicing A/R's to sales or production, increasing inventory, or other growth-inducing moves (see Preface, "Business Owners' Comments about Factoring"). This doubling of sales may be higher or lower than the actual effect on your company's business; the trick is to gauge as accurately as you can how much more business you could gain, and what your revised costs would be.

	Before Factoring	With Factoring
Gross Revenues	100,000	200,000
Cost of Goods Sold	60,000	120,000
Gross Profits	40,000	80,000
Less:		
Variable Expenses	15,000	30,000
Fixed Expenses	20,000	20,000
Overhead	35,000	50,000
Cost of Factoring	0	8,000
Total Expenses	35,000	58,000
Net Profit	5,000	22,000

Summary

Net Profit After Factoring:	22,000
Net Profit Before Factoring:	5,000
Additional Profit from Factoring:	17,000

Now when the company factors its receivables, the cash on hand enables Gross Revenues to increase to $200,000, and COGS and Gross Profit correspond to this increase. The Variable Expenses also increase to correspond with the added volume, but Fixed Expenses remain the same. Fixed Expenses may include rent, utilities, and other expenses that will change little or not at all as a result of increased business. Add new Variable Expenses to Fixed Expenses and you'll see that while Overhead increases in dollars, it actually decreases in proportion to Profits.

Now, this company also has a new expense – the Cost of Factoring. At a 4% rate of the $200,000 factored, your Total Expenses have increased from $35,000 to $58,000. However, with the significant increase in sales and the maintenance of Fixed Costs at the same level both before and with factoring, the bottom line has significantly improved. The Cost of Factoring has not just paid for itself, but made a big difference in profitability.

Will every company that factors experience this kind of improvement? Of course not. The key question for your company is, "How much could my company make if it had an unlimited supply of cash on hand?" Perhaps you could double revenues as in the above example; perhaps you would make less, perhaps more. At any rate, make some projections, insert your company's realistic figures into this simple example, run the numbers, and see if factoring makes sense. If it does, you might ask: "Can my business afford *not* to factor?"

Other Advantages of Factoring

Earlier the statement was made that factoring is not a loan; it is the sale of an asset. Why is this important? A loan places a debt on your balance sheet and costs interest. By contrast, factoring puts money in the bank without creating any obligation to pay it back. How? You haven't *borrowed money,* you've *sold an asset* – your receivables. This has provided more cash on hand and no debt you are obligated to repay with interest, which in turn strengthens your balance sheet.

What's more, anyone who has borrowed money (or tried to) knows loans are largely dependent on the borrower's financial soundness. Banks and traditional lenders require a business to be in existence for a minimum of two to three years, and sometimes even more. If you can't come up with two or three years of income tax statements, not to mention financial statements (going back at least that far) that show financial strength, banks will not lend to you.

However, while factors are interested in your business experience and how well you run your company, they're most interested in the strength and creditworthiness of your customers. Why? Quite simply, your *customers* are the ones paying for the invoices the factor purchases. This is the big difference between lenders and factors.

Banks rely exclusively on the borrower's strength; factors rely primarily on the paying customers' strength. This is a real plus for new businesses without an established track record, or who have poor credit, or who even have been through bankruptcy. These "automatic killers" for those seeking bank loans are not necessarily so for factoring clients, as long as their customers are quite strong. Because the focus is more on the customers than the company needing the money, factors often welcome clients that banks turn away. In fact, bank leads – from loan officers referring declined loan applicants – provide factors some of their best prospects for new business.

What's more, factoring is directly linked to your company's sales. The more sales you make, the more cash you can have immediately available by selling your invoices. Thus factoring enables you to tap into funds that are restricted only by your ability to generate further business with creditworthy customers. As the subtitle of this book says, factoring your good receivables enables your company to obtain literally *unlimited funds without a loan.*

The History of Factoring

To the surprise of most people, factoring has been practiced for centuries. The ancient Phoenicians supposedly used a primitive form of factoring, and the Romans were known to sell promissory notes at a discount. The word "factor" itself comes from Latin, the language of Rome. It means "to do" or "to make." Our word "factory" comes from the same root, and everyone knows a factory is a building "where things are made." Our dictionary says "factor" in Latin means "doer" – and we might say factors are "business doers" – they make business happen.

The Pilgrims' journeys to America were financed by advances from a factor who provided the funds to pay for passage. They repaid this money with earnings in their new home which they sent back to England.

Over time as the colonies grew, a London businessman sold raw materials (timber and furs) the colonists provided to English businesses. He guaranteed the colonists' credit for buying refined goods they needed from England, and collected the colonists' payments to the London merchants. He kept a fee for his efforts, and a colonial form of factoring was established.

Down through the years factoring has continued in England and throughout Europe, where it is a common business practice today. Most Europeans are familiar with the procedure, unlike many Americans who have never heard of it. Despite this widespread lack of awareness here, factoring is quite prevalent in the American economy and well known to large businesses, many of whom became large through factoring their receivables.

Factoring as we now know it in the U.S. began to be commonly practiced in the garment industry in New York City in the early 20th Century, and has continued so to this day. Virtually all companies who manufacture clothing utilize factors and began their business doing so.

Up until the 1980's factoring transactions were limited to rather large volume clients. However, with the savings and loan problems that occurred during that decade, banks became more tightly regulated. Business loans to small and medium sized businesses became harder to acquire. That restriction to the money supply made factoring one of the few financing alternatives for smaller businesses, and factors emerged who were willing to take on smaller businesses than larger factors would accept.

During the 1990's, many factors were funding receivables larger than $10,000 per month in invoice volume. This continues to be the case and businesses with steady factoring volumes of $20,000 per month or more who have very reliable customers should be able to find a factor interested in purchasing their receivables.

With the economic difficulties that started in 2008, bank lending to small businesses constricted considerably and obtaining a business loan became very difficult if not impossible. This brought awareness of factoring to many business owners who were previously unacquainted with it and made factoring more mainstream, because (just as during good economic times) factors were the only source from which a business could obtain funding. Even with economic recovery, banks cannot finance many companies needing capital. Factoring continues to be needed, and will be used for years to come.

Factors willing to purchase small receivables (those under $10,000 to $15,000 in monthly volume) are present though in less number than those funding the $25,000, $50,000, or $100,000 monthly range. These very small factors are steadily emerging.

Some of these very small factors are entrepreneurs who want to operate small businesses of their own, and factoring appeals to them. Others are people who factor on a part-time basis who may have other businesses complimentary to their factoring service, such as an accountant, attorney, or those who broker larger factoring accounts. Still others are private investors with steady jobs who factor small numbers of clients as an alternative means of investing.

Later we will consider what to look for in a factor in terms of your capital needs and the services factors provide. For now, be assured that there are factors available to fund just about every size of business – from those needing to factor just a few thousand dollars per month to those factoring millions, and everything in between.

Factoring: Sell Your Invoices Today, Get Cash Tomorrow

3
Why Haven't I Heard of This Before?

After reading the previous chapter, seeing how factoring can help so many businesses, and learning of factoring's long history, a logical question comes to mind: "If factoring is so prevalent and answers the financing needs of so many businesses, why don't more people know about it?" More to the point, "Why haven't *I* heard of this before?"

For better or worse, factoring is one of the best-kept secrets from the general public in this country. Because of its modern origins in New York City's garment industry, factoring grew up in a rather tough environment. The association with this atmosphere may influence the feelings that some financial professionals have about the factoring industry.

For some time factoring was considered the financing means of last resort. That is, when bank loans were much more easily obtained than they are today, companies who could not obtain them were somewhat suspect. Then as now, factoring was used by companies who could not obtain bank loans. Loans were not available to them because of their poor business practices, they were on the verge of bankruptcy, or they were otherwise deemed to be in poor financial condition and therefore high risk. They were forced to pay high factoring rates just to stay afloat, and companies who factored were looked upon as "sinking ships," undesirable because banks would not touch them.

Today, the banking environment has changed considerably. Since the savings and loan crisis of the 1980's, the economic and political nervousness after 9/11, and the widespread constriction of bank lending starting in 2008, obtaining (and even keeping) a bank loan or line of credit has not been easy, even for existing businesses. Many companies with bank loans or lines had them cut or lost them completely despite the fact their business remained sound.

Factoring costs remains higher than those of traditional bank loans for the same reasons they always have: factors fund the businesses banks turn away. Because factors have always accepted clients that banks decline and because factors always face the risk of financial loss, factoring discounts are naturally higher than traditional lending rates. However, as we'll see in the coming pages, comparing factoring rates to bank interest is to compare apples to oranges, and tends to overlook the key question: will factoring *make* a business more money than it *costs?* If the answer is yes, the cost of factoring becomes rather unimportant.

Unfortunately (and perhaps unfairly), factoring rates are generally looked upon by some in the financial world as being unacceptably high. In particular, accountants and sometimes bankers and attorneys consider factoring costs to be too pricey to be worthy of their recommendation, especially when traditional lending rates are quite low. For this reason, professionals who are in a position to inform business owners of this alternative means of financing their businesses when bank loans are not available, often do not do so.

This omission may occur because these professionals perceive the cost as "too high," or simply because they don't fully understand factoring themselves. Most college and university business programs do not teach classes on factoring. At most, the practice is only casually mentioned but rarely explored in depth. Thus, those trained to be business or financial experts often have little or no exposure to the practice of factoring, and don't completely understand it themselves.

Unfortunately, the perceived "high" cost of factoring begs the question of obtaining funding for most new or young companies. The vast majority of businesses fail within their first five years of existence, and many argue the most common reason those fail is due to lack of capital. Most businesses just can't get the money they need to operate. If more young and startup companies had access to adequate capital, more would be likely to succeed.

Obtaining financing – from any source – is now commonly accepted by business owners as a requirement to maintain operations. For example, many small startup companies begin with their owners borrowing money from credit cards – a practice unheard of a few decades ago.

Factoring can provide the funding a business owner needs while making the business more profitable. Put in simple words, if factoring costs less than the income it generates, *and* improves a company's bottom line, *and* increases its production, *and* enables growth... so what if it's "more expensive" than a bank loan? Factoring has helped the business owner not only get his company started and kept his company going, factoring has enabled it to thrive. "Less costly" banks loans are worth zero to businesses that can't obtain them in the first place. And bank loans' inaccessibility to very small businesses continues to be the rule, not the exception.

Unfortunately, finance professionals' silence is often based on a lack of understanding of exactly how factoring works, the advantages it provides, and the relative cost in light of its benefits. When a business simply *cannot* obtain a bank loan or line, an SBA loan, venture capital, or angel investors, factoring is usually the *only* form of funding available. Thus, financial and other professionals who intentionally do not inform business owners of factoring's availability, due to their own ignorance or outdated assumptions, do a disservice to their clients.

With the difficult economy and more small factors emerging, factoring is available to smaller and smaller companies and has entered the mainstream for very small businesses as it did for large corporations. Factoring has become familiar to a larger number of people, and thereby gained even further acceptance as a legitimate and even valuable form of business finance. The use of factoring also strengthens the business environment as a whole, as more and more small businesses are able to obtain the capital they need to survive their infancy and grow to maturity.

Imagine just for a moment the effect on our nation's economy if a vast number of small and startup companies had access to all the operating capital they needed to grow. What would happen if hundreds of thousands and even millions of small companies could obtain *unlimited funds without a loan?*

Part 2

Learning More

Factoring: Sell Your Invoices Today, Get Cash Tomorrow

4
Factoring Versus Other Financing

Who Can Utilize Factoring

While factoring can help many business owners and executives who currently do not use it, factoring does not work for *every* type of business. Companies who receive cash or credit card payments in full, and who do not wish to expand to customers requiring net 15 or 30 day terms, do not need to factor. Also, companies which sell exclusively to consumers will not be able to use the services of a traditional factor (although consumer finance companies exist to help such businesses). Therefore, such businesses as restaurants, most retail stores, online auction businesses, and the like cannot ordinarily make use of factoring.[1]

Yet requirements for factoring are uncomplicated, and as we've seen, somewhat different from traditional business financing. Any company who wishes to improve its cash flow with factoring must meet two simple criteria. The company must:

1. Have verifiable invoices to creditworthy business or government customers.

2. Wait a period of time to receive payment for these invoices. Usually waiting about two weeks to two months is the

---

[1] However, many finance companies provide cash advances based on future credit card sales. Businesses with credit card sales to anyone, including consumers, can benefit from this type of funding.

optimal period of time, though some companies will factor invoices that are paid in less or more time than this.

These are the "bare bones" requirements for any factor to provide funding. Beyond this, each factor will have requirements unique to his business that will reflect a factoring niche and dollar volume of clients' receivables.

How can you determine if factoring will enrich your business? If any of the following describe your company and you have good invoices to sell, factoring will provide at least one benefit. The greater the number of these statements that describe your company, the more factoring will offer you.

- Financing is unavailable to pay operating expenses.

- Your company is growing.

- Your company is new or relatively young (in operation less than three to five years).

- Your company is a small- or medium-sized business which sells to larger or more established customers.

- Your company has a negative net worth but sells to creditworthy customers.

- You frequently or occasionally have inadequate cash on hand to purchase materials and/or meet payroll.

- You are turning away business that requires terms of 15 days or more.

- Your company would benefit from having additional working capital.

- You delay paying bills because of poor cash flow, which is damaging your credit standing.

- You could save costs by taking advantage of vendor discounts for cash.

- You need professional management of your billing and/or Accounts Receivable in order to give closer attention to sales and/or product or service delivery.

- You need professional collection and credit analysis services.

Factoring Compared
to Traditional Financing

When most business owners seek financing, traditional sources they usually seek first are their own funds and those of private investors, then bank loans, and finally venture capital. Let's compare factoring to each of these as well as to other alternatives.

Private Investors

1. Equity

Private Investors. Most startup businesses begin with private investment from the owner's personal resources, and/or those of relatives, friends, past business associates, and perhaps angel investors. When the owner's personal funds (and often credit card limits) are exhausted, he looks to people he knows who might be willing to help. In most cases, those funds eventually run dry so the business owner, if he hasn't already, will often give up substantial amounts of equity to obtain more money. As these funds are used and additional funds are needed to keep the business going, more equity may be demanded by private investors.

Over time, the business owner not only has accumulated a heavy debt load, he may well have lost majority ownership of his company. This may also cause friction between the owner and investor/s who may differ in their perspectives as to how the company should be run.

Factoring. Many factors welcome startup companies and especially desire those with excellent growth potential. Because the factor's income is tied to the factored receivables of a client, both the factor and client increase their income as the client's business grows. Meanwhile the business owner maintains full ownership of his company. As mentioned above, factors do not seek a stake in nor control of a client's company. While factors want a client's business

41

to run smoothly and they can often offer valuable advice, the business owner maintains control and full business ownership.

2. Availability of Funds

Private Investors. Often private funds from all known resources of the owner eventually are exhausted, and other means of financing must be sought. The larger a business grows, the more difficult finding private investors can become. Doing so means a deeper hole and further debt.

Factoring. While an extremely small factor's resources may be somewhat limited, most factors will be able to accommodate a client's growth. If a client grows too large for a very small factor to fund, larger factors are available and usually quite willing to step in. What's more, because the factoring volume has become larger, somewhat lower discounts may be available when making the transition to a larger factor.

After factoring over some period of time, a company's cash flow will often stabilize and factoring may no longer be needed. If a business owner desires a lower cost bank loan, she may now be in a position to qualify for one.

Nonetheless, many business owners choose to continue factoring to take advantage of the extra services they have come to appreciate from their factor: Accounts Receivable management, billing services, credit screening and guidance, collection services, and more. The chapter "What to Look for in a Factor" describes these services in greater detail.

Bank Loans

1. Application

Banks. To obtain a loan, business owners are typically required to provide at least two or three year's worth of tax returns and business financials, including Income Statements and Balance Sheets. Companies who have not been in business this long, and therefore cannot provide these documents, need not even apply because they will be turned down at their first inquiry.

Business plans are commonly required and some banks will demand the loan applicant be their banking customer for quite some time, maintaining checking or savings accounts, Certificates of Deposit, and other banking products. This gives the bank time to assess fiscal habits and patterns which assists them in determining the level of risk associated with lending money. However, being a bank customer in no way obligates the bank to provide a loan, and even bank customers of many years' standing cannot expect their business loan applications to be approved. Many are not.

Factoring. Companies who wish to factor larger volumes will often be required to provide tax returns and business financials. Factors of smaller businesses often do not have such a requirement. Many factors welcome new and startup companies who obviously will not have such documentation.

While larger factors may require a business plan, most small and medium sized factors do not. Because most prospective clients will have no previous experience with a particular factor, requirements for using that factor's service do not exist.

Factors will expect clients to complete some legal agreements in order to secure their funds. Because factors take risk on a regular basis, they naturally need to take precautions to minimize this risk. The paperwork you might expect from most factors is discussed in detail in the chapter, "Signing On," and is less complicated than that for bank loans.

2. Re-applying for More Funds

Banks. When a borrower needs additional funds beyond a loan already granted, he must re-apply for another loan. Like the first time around, the same paperwork will be required and will again take weeks or even months to learn of approval.

Factoring. Once a factoring account is established, receiving a new advance is simply a matter of supplying new invoices. Customers need to be approved only once to obtain future advances for invoices to them.

3. Credit Standing

Banks. Any applicant who has poor or questionable credit can expect to have their loan declined. Likewise, those who have declared bankruptcy just once can routinely expect to be refused financing from a bank. And people with records of criminal convictions, judgments, and other negative public record information will not find bank loans available to them.

Factoring. Like banks, factors will perform due diligence when setting up new accounts. Public records will be searched for liens, judgments, bankruptcies, and criminal history. Criminal history will usually disqualify an applicant from factoring, and a history of judgments, tax liens, and uncollected debts usually lead a factor to decline an applicant.

A bankruptcy and lower credit standing are usually less of a concern as long as the company's customers' credit is solid. If a company has UCC (Uniform Commercial Code) liens filed on its assets, particularly in which its receivables are held as collateral, these will need to be worked out before factoring can commence. If they can't be, a factor will usually decline an application. These liens are often held by banks if a prospective client has a loan or line of credit; the bank may or may not be willing to subordinate its position to a factor. UCC liens are explained in further detail later in this chapter and in the chapter "Signing On."

If a tax lien is in place or a client is in bankruptcy, a factor may be able to help the client through this by working with tax authorities or a bankruptcy trustee to make regular required payments, taken from client advances.

While many factoring clients begin their relationship with a factor with marginal credit, factoring can help improve their credit standing. By having adequate cash on hand to pay bills promptly, companies can see gradual improvements to their credit rating because they pay their bills on time.

4. Repayment

Banks. Business loans are typically paid back in amortized monthly payments which include principal and interest, much like house or car payments. They are often for a period of seven years. Interest is based on the client's credit rating and current prime rate.

Factoring. Because factoring is not a loan, there are no principal or interest payments to make. Discounts are paid (rather than interest charged) based on the client's industry, customer's credit standing, size and volume of the receivables, and the length of time customers take to pay. These discounts are retained by the factor when customer payments are received and/or deducted from advances, so there is no added work involved in paying a factor.

Some factors will require clients to factor a minimum dollar volume of invoices each month for a specific number of months, particularly if a bankruptcy or tax lien is involved. If this volume is not met, minimum charges are collected. However, many factors have neither monthly minimums nor term contracts. This gives their clients great control over the accounts they factor and the discounts they pay.

5. Collateral

Banks. When providing a loan or line of credit, banks routinely require collateral be provided which at least equals and usually exceeds the amount of money borrowed. This collateral is secured with a UCC filing with the Secretary of State, which places a lien on the collateral and gives the bank first rights to the collateral in the event of default.

Usually all assets of a company, and often personal assets of the business owner, are required as collateral. These personal assets are secured by a personal guarantee, which stipulates the borrower is required to pay back the debt from personal assets if the business defaults on the loan.

Factoring. Factors also routinely file a UCC lien, and like banks, will require they be in first position with these filings. Collateral will usually consist of at least the accounts receivable of the company, while other assets are often included as well.

Some factors require personal guarantees to be signed as part of their security; some do not.

5. Compensating Balances

Banks. Some bank loans and lines of credit require compensating balances. These are the funds a business is required to keep in a deposit or reserve account, apart from the loan. It acts as on-hand collateral for the bank and helps offset what the bank perceives as risk. It is also a means of yield enhancement for the lender, making the effective interest rate of a loan higher than the stated interest rate.

Collateral requirements and compensating balances often lead to a common complaint by those turned away by banks: the people who qualify for loans are those who don't need them, and those who need loans don't qualify. One also is reminded of this joke...

Question: What is a banker?
Answer: Someone who offers you an umbrella when the sun is shining, then takes it away when it starts to rain.

Factoring. Factors do not require compensating balances or reserve funds to be on hand to begin factoring. Reserves may be built up over time and can be tapped in the case of customer nonpayment, but they are not necessary at the onset of factoring.

Venture Capital

1. Business Plan

Venture Capital. Venture Capital companies routinely demand thorough and detailed business plans before providing funds. Future financial projections are expected, as are sophisticated market analyses and marketing strategies. Extended experience and unique expertise on the part of business management is expected as well.

Venture capital firms receive a large number of professionally created business plans that represent months, even years, of preparation. Yet despite these painstaking efforts, the percentage of projects actually funded with venture capital is extremely low. In difficult economic times, venture capital can virtually dry up and disappear.

Factoring. Very few factoring companies require a prospective client to provide a business plan. If one is already on hand, it will be welcomed and studied. Yet preparing a business plan is generally not needed for businesses wishing to factor their receivables.

2. Equity

Venture Capital. Venture capitalists will require a significant share of equity in any business they fund. This may be majority ownership from the outset, or a minority stake to begin. However, future cash infusions will demand additional equity shares. Venture firms frequently expect to control a funded company and place hand-picked staff in key management positions. Business owners who wish to maintain complete control of their firms cannot consider venture capital as a means of financing.

Factoring. Factors do not want to gain control of businesses they fund. While they can provide expert guidance and management of important receivables functions, controlling a client's company is not their desire. A factor has his or her own company to run, and prefers to generate income from discounts, not equity.

Government Programs

1. Application

Many government programs are intended to help small and what are sometimes referred to as "disadvantaged" businesses, which are minority- or women-owned. SBA loans are administered by local banks and regulated by the government. That means such funds for which you might apply are controlled by someone with a banker's frame of reference who must conform to government regulations. Does that sound like a "borrower-friendly" arrangement?

The requirements for meeting any of these programs are fairly restrictive. Most do not provide large sums of money and like any government-related funding, require the patience of Job to wade through the initial paperwork... wait...fill out more paperwork...wait...and after several months...learn your application has (probably) been declined.

If you have an immediate need for cash, waiting for these loans (which must be paid back) can literally be a business killer. I can't count the number of exasperated (and often nearly desperate) small business owners who have sought factoring after experiencing nothing but frustration in applying for these programs.

47

2. Re-applying for More Funds

Same story as the bank, second verse. When a borrower needs additional funds beyond a loan already granted, she must re-apply for another loan. Like the first time around, the same paperwork will be required and will again take weeks or even months to learn of approval. Do you really want to go through all that again for $25,000 – if you were lucky enough to get it the first time?

3. Repayment

Government programs, like business loans, create debt and typically are paid back in amortized monthly principal and interest payments.

Factoring. Everything described about factoring in the section on Bank Loans applies in this section. Applying for factoring is a breeze compared to applying and waiting for government programs, and there is no need to re-apply for more funds once your account is established. Finally, you have nothing to repay because you're not borrowing money, but selling an asset.

Equipment Leasing

Generally, equipment leasing can help businesses with cash in two ways:

1. When a business needs equipment, a leasing company purchases the equipment – computers, machinery, vehicles, what have you – then leases it to a client, who makes a monthly lease payment, much like leasing a car. The advantage is that you don't have large capital outlays for such purchases, and obsolescence isn't your problem. Having this equipment can enable you to take on new jobs or customers without large cash outlays.

   This can often work hand-in-hand with factoring, as long as the factor and leasing company are not placing a lien on the same collateral, which is usually not a problem. Leasing companies want to lien the equipment leased, while factors want to lien the company's receivables.

2. If you need cash and already own equipment that has value, some leasing companies will provide a lease buy-back arrangement.

That is, you sell them your equipment for a lump sum of cash, then make monthly lease payments as you continue to use the equipment.

Factors and leasing companies often work side-by-side. Both target the same market (companies needing funds) and offer complementary products which don't really compete with each other. Factors provide cash for any business need, leasing companies provide cash for equipment, or the equipment itself. Both make their income from strengthening clients' businesses.

In fact, some factoring companies offer leasing products, and some leasing companies factor receivables on a limited basis. If you are currently factoring and think leasing could further help your business, your factor will probably be able to make a referral. Likewise, if you are using a leasing company and would like to factor, ask your leasing agent for the name of a good factor who handles a company your size.

5

Faulty Assumptions and Mistakes to Avoid

While factoring is a simple concept, people frequently make incorrect assumptions or repeat those they've heard. Let's look at the most common.

"Isn't Factoring Expensive?"

As discussed earlier, the cost of factoring is generally higher than traditional forms of financing. However, when those traditional forms are unavailable (as they are to a vast number of businesses), the issue of factoring's comparable higher cost becomes moot. When asked the common question, "Isn't factoring expensive?" a reasonable answer is, "Compared to what? Loans you can't get?"

The significant question for companies considering factoring is not, "How much does factoring cost?" but "Will factoring generate more income than it costs?" If the answer is yes, the decision to factor is one of simple arithmetic and becomes a sound business decision. Refer back to the example in the section "The Difference Factoring Makes" in the chapter "What Is Factoring?" If your bottom line is strengthened by factoring, why would you choose *not* to factor?

Frequently business owners (and invariably, their accountants) look at the amount they are being charged in factoring discounts and attempt to annualize what they call the "interest." This leads to some shaky conclusions because they're making the proverbial comparison of apples (receiving bank loans and paying interest) to oranges (selling receivables and paying discounts).

For example, suppose a factor is charging a 4% factoring discount for 30 days. The temptation is to annualize this discount by multiplying 4% by 12, resulting in the gasped question, "You're going to charge me *48% interest?!"*

Having been asked this question many times, the factor will patiently ask the business owner if he accepts 2 Net 10 terms. In other words, if a customer pays in 10 days, does this business owner give a 2% discount? Many do…and when they do, often receive payments long after the 10 days have come and gone, yet the 2% discount is taken anyway. Let's run the same numbers with such terms.

In a year there are 36 ten-day periods. If these 10 day discounts are calculated for an annual rate, these businesses are paying 2% x 36, or 72% annually, for payments made in 10 days. Do business owners and accountants therefore acknowledge they are paying 72% interest on such transactions? "No," they reason. "I'm discounting for cash, not paying interest." Using the same reasoning, factoring expenses are also discounts for cash – not annualized interest. Thus we see why the loan vs. factoring comparison is "apples to oranges."

Moreover, how does factoring compare to 2 Net 10 terms – both of which are discounts for cash? Factoring discounts are usually *less* than the terms most business owners are already willing to extend fast paying customers – and never think twice about extending. Furthermore, factoring advances are usually received within one to two business days. "Quick" payments for the higher 2 Net 10 terms typically take the full ten days to arrive.

Again, the correct question is not, "What is the interest you're charging?" because that's simply a red herring. The correct question is, "Can I take the cash generated from factoring and use it to earn more than I'm paying for it?" If the answer is no, factoring will not benefit you. If the answer is yes, why would you decline to factor?

If factoring will increase your bottom line, deciding not to factor will actually cost your company money. In the sample manufacturing company's comparison cited earlier, not factoring would have cost the business $17,000 in missed opportunities. Why would someone do this? Probably because his accountant told him factoring was "too expensive." You be the judge.

"My Profit Margins Are Too Narrow"

Some industries have slim profit margins. If a company's margins are 4%, and its factoring discounts are 3 to 5%, the owner may understandably assume factoring will drive him in the red. This is true if sales volumes remain the same with factoring.

However, if sales jump with increased cash flow as they did in the earlier example, factoring can again more than pay for itself. You simply have to run the numbers and see if the cost of factoring will be less than the increased profit. The cost of factoring plays a crucial role in such circumstances.

What's more, there is value to the extra services a factor offers. If using these services (billing, A/R collections follow-up, credit screening, and so on) enables you to eliminate these tasks from in-house staff, you'll lower your expenses and/or give your staff other responsibilities. This can improve your profit margin in addition to increasing sales. Therefore you need to consider not only the costs of factoring, but the benefits as well.

"Won't a Factor Make Higher Discounts from Slow Payments?"

Because slower customer payments result in increased discounts the client pays (and the factor receives), many people assume there is little incentive for factors to desire or encourage fast payments from customers. They reason that factors will have little interest in urging prompt customer payment. Let's take a look at this assumption and see why it is quite erroneous.

First of all, the longer any invoice takes to pay the greater the likelihood it will become uncollectible. Obviously non-recourse factors will not want this because when that happens they will absorb a loss. Recourse factors don't want this either because of the extra time (translate money) they must spend trying to collect.

If the client (to whom the recourse factor turns when a customer does not pay) has difficulty repaying the funds or cannot provide a new invoice to replace the unpaid one, the recourse factor may suffer a loss just like the non-recourse factor. Obviously all factors prefer solid, dependably paying customers any day over those who are inconsistent or just flaky.

Second, while factoring discounts increase over time, factors prefer to "turn" their money as often as possible. That is, they will prefer to make their discounts on 30-day payment turns, rather than those that turn in 60 or 90 days. Why?

For one thing, their money is more secure, as just described. Also, when you look closely at discount rates and do the math, factors often actually make less the longer a customer takes to pay. Let's look at a few scenarios.

Let's say Factor A charges 4% for the first 30 days, and 1% for each 10 days after that. This factor's discount rates look like this:

# Days	Discount
0-30	4%
31-40	5%
41-50	6%
51-60	7%
61-70	8%
71-80	9%
81-90	10%

If a $1,000 invoice pays within 30 days, the factor earns $40 in discounts. If it pays in 40 days, the factor earns 5%, or $50. If the invoice pays in 60 days, the factor makes 7%, or $70. If the invoice pays in 90 days, the factor makes 10%. So why wouldn't the factor want the invoices to take as long as possible to pay and therefore make the higher discounts?

The answer is simple. This factor will make more when invoices pay quickly than when they pay slowly. The above discounts (which are not uncommon) will earn Factor A more if he can buy three $1,000 invoices that each pay in 30 days than if he buys one $1,000 invoice that pays in 90 days. That is, buying three invoices in sequence that each pay in 30 days will result in discounts of 4% + 4% + 4% = 12% total. Buying only one invoice that pays in 90 days will result in a total discount 10%. Which would you prefer?

What's more, if payment was expected in 30 days but received in 90, the factor probably made phone calls to check on the status of the payment. This is common procedure when an invoice is overdue, and because this takes staff time, there is increased cost to the factor...not to mention concern over whether this will become a bad debt and potential loss. So Factor A will prefer to turn his money three times in 90 days instead of turning the same money once in that 90 day period. No brainer.

Let's say Factor B has rates in which the discounts are consistent over a period of time, ensuring she will make the same discount over time rather than less, unlike Factor A. Such discount rates could look like this:

# Days	Discount
0-30	4%
31-45	6%
46-60	8%
61-75	10%
76-90	12%

If a $1,000 invoice to Factor B pays within 30 days, she earns $40 in discounts. If it pays in 60 days, the factor earns 8%, or $80. If the invoice pays in 90 days, she makes 12%, or $120. In other words, Factor B makes the same amount buying one invoice that pays in 90 days as she does buying three invoices that each pay in 30 days.

Will she prefer the slower paying invoice? Of course not: there is no benefit in waiting longer to be paid and the risk of nonpayment remains higher with the one slow payment than it does with the three faster payments. Factor B will prefer the faster paying invoices just like Factor A.

While there is a myriad of factoring discounts and breakdowns in the increment of days as to how they are calculated, the above logic holds for practically all of them. That means factors (just like their clients) will prefer fast paying invoices over slow paying invoices. Their risk is lower and discount income either the same or higher.

"I Thought My Bad Credit Didn't Matter"

As mentioned earlier, factors are more concerned with the credit of your customers than yours, the client. Many companies who are turned down by banks due to dings in their credit are often accepted by a factor. However that doesn't mean that every client who applies with absolutely atrocious credit is going to be approved.

True, a single bankruptcy usually does not automatically disqualify you from factoring, as it does a bank loan. A history of paying your bills very slowly and long beyond terms can also lead a banker to show you the door, while a factor may understand this is caused by a cash flow problem that factoring can solve.

On the other hand, factors do look for clients who, despite a poor credit score, still exhibit personal characteristics of honesty, integrity, dependability, and hard work. But a past history of criminal behavior (fraud, robbery, embezzlement, and such) will quickly disqualify you with a factor just as it will a banker. Likewise a history indicating you don't follow through on obligations or live a responsible life are also likely to disqualify you: nonpayment of child support, more than one DUI, consistent tax lien filings year after year, and the like. The occasional speeding or parking ticket won't make any difference to factors, but more serious infractions that call your character into question are red flags to any factor. Factors seek to fund companies who are in need of improved cash flow and who may be in a jam, but whose owners are honest, decent, trustworthy individuals.

For example, I once had a prospect apply to factor with my company. He didn't indicate he had a poor credit record as some applicants warn ahead of time; he just applied and waited for my response.

During the underwriting, I discovered he not only had bad credit and a few bankruptcies; he had page after page after page – probably at least a hundred instances – of collection companies who had written off his account as uncollectible. These ranged from relatively small debts of less than $50 to considerably larger amounts of several thousands of dollars each. The presence of so many similar and negative experiences told me that he functioned in life by obtaining credit he couldn't (or never intended) to pay back, then walked away from his obligations and ignored those who attempted to make him pay bills he legitimately owed. I knew all too well that if I factored his invoices, sooner or later I would end up in the same position as all these unfortunate companies he had waltzed out on.

When I informed him his application was declined and the reason was the numerous write offs by collection agencies on his credit report, he indignantly responded, "But I thought my bad credit didn't matter." Needless to say, in his case it did.

Just like anyone else, factors don't want to work with deadbeats with no sense of responsibility. A few dents in your credit won't usually disqualify you from factoring; a horrendous trail of carnage like this person left will eliminate you immediately.

Right and Wrong Accounts to Factor

Many people new to factoring make the assumption that the best invoices to factor are those which are slowest to pay. Actually, the best invoices to factor are those which are paid in about 30 to 45 days, and those which are paid in about two weeks to two months are usually appropriate as well.

However, invoices that routinely take 90 or 120 days or even longer are typically not the best to factor. Why? As we've just seen, the longer an invoice takes to pay, the higher the likelihood that it will not be paid at all.

Especially if you factor on a recourse basis, factoring customers whom you know from experience are poor-paying or non-paying, can be a ticking time bomb. Obtaining the cash advances will no doubt help you in the short run, but what happens when the recourse period is reached and the payment hasn't arrived? Now you owe the factor for the advance you received *plus* the discount (sizeable by this time). How will you pay this? In short, factoring poor-paying customers makes your cash flow even worse in the long run.

Factoring works best when the invoices you sell are to dependable, stable, creditworthy customers. These are the customers who don't pay you immediately, but will definitely pay you. If your customer is financially shaky or has been slippery about payments in the past, your invoices to him are not good candidates for factoring.

Factors are not collection companies who thrive on deadbeat payers. Factors are financiers who invest in dependable payments coming from solid companies. They do not want to purchase bad debt. Therefore if you have uncollectable accounts which are long overdue and/or you expect to have problems receiving payment, the proper move is to give them to a collection agency – not a factor.

On the other hand, customers who pay immediately or within a week or so are usually not worth factoring, unless your need for cash is urgent and you receive excellent short-term factoring rates. When you receive payments this quickly, the factoring discount you pay is probably not worth the short wait to receive your quick-paying customer payments. This is especially true if your discount starts on a 0 to 30 day basis, as many do. If your discount starts on a daily basis or on a basis of 7, 10 or 15 days, however, quick-paying accounts that take a week or two to arrive may be beneficial to factor.

Likewise, if your customer pays with a credit card, your merchant account payments should come in quickly enough to meet your cash flow needs. Credit card costs are usually less than factoring discounts, so there is no need to replace credit card transactions with a factor. Credit cards, in essence, are factored accounts with fairly low costs to you, the merchant.

Therefore, when a desirable account will not pay with credit cards yet demands 30 day terms, factoring such a customer makes sense. Thus, accepting credit cards for consumer and some government and business accounts, in tandem with factoring for other government and business accounts, make a great combination and can greatly improve your cash flow.

Right and Wrong Reasons to Factor

If your company is on the brink of disaster and you want to factor to save a sinking ship, factoring may not be the best answer. So how do you know if you *shouldn't* factor? Answer this simple question: "How will I use the cash I obtain from factoring?"

If selling your receivables will increase your volume of business by increasing production capability and/or creating more sales, you are probably using factoring for the right reasons. But if you want to use the cash only to pay off bad debts, pay past due cost-of-goods invoices you owe, and catch up on severely delinquent overhead costs, factoring may not be the answer.

Factoring is a tool, just like the hammer and saw in your workshop. You don't use a saw to drive a nail, nor a hammer to cut a piece of wood. They work best when used for the job for which they were created. Likewise, the tool of factoring is a dependable and time-honored means of growing and expanding a business. Used for the wrong job, it won't solve your problem and can leave you further frustrated. But when factoring is used for the proper job – stabilizing cash flow, company growth and expansion – you will be amazed at how well it can work.

Mistakes to Avoid

As you have no doubt realized by now, factors are subject to the risks of nonpayment and even fraud in the course of doing business. Be assured they are keenly aware of the risks they take. Therefore factors are careful to take precautions against fraudulent activity from their clients and clients' customers. The two most common forms of fraud factors face are purchasing fraudulent invoices and conversion of payment checks. Let me explain each of these.

Fraudulent Invoices

Your factoring contract will no doubt include a provision that states the invoices you sell are legitimate, non-consumer, and unencumbered. In other words, you're selling paper that contains correct information as to your customer, your product or service, and the amount due. You're not generating invoices with no basis in reality, nor "doctoring" the information on them in any way. Everything on them is true and verifiable.

What's more, you're stating there are no offsets – that is, you don't owe your customer money which will be deducted from his payment for the invoice. The amount on the invoice is the amount your customer is going to pay. Factors take precautions to verify the validity of invoices.

The need for trust is inherent in any factoring relationship and key to growing your company with a factor. If a business owner sells invoices which are inaccurate (and when the inaccuracy is intentional, therefore fraudulent) he is violating that trust. Always be honest and make absolutely sure all your factored invoices are accurate so the trust is maintained and your business can continue to grow. Clients who intentionally factor fraudulent invoices are committing criminal behavior and are subject to serious penalties.

Redirecting Payments and Conversion of Checks

The other most common fraudulent activity factoring clients may commit is to convert customer checks which pay factored invoices. In other words, instead of a check going to the factor, the business owner obtains a customer's check for a factored invoice and deposits or cashes it. This may be done quite accidentally and innocently, especially if an employee picks up the mail and/or makes bank deposits, but isn't involved in tracking factored accounts.

However, by redirecting electronic payments or converting checks – whether by intentionally re-directing the payment address or simply receiving and keeping funds paying a factored invoice – that business owner is keeping money that is not his. He has confiscated a payment (which is now the factor's money) without the factor's knowledge or permission. Some may justify this action with the excuse that they "just really need it" or are using it "for an emergency" and intend to pay the factor back soon. But no matter how dire the need or pure the intent to repay, this is fraud and a breach of contract that will (at best) immediately erode your factor's trust in you. Simply put, this is a criminal action.

Lack of Cooperation

You and your factor in many ways are partners in business. Your factor's funds enable your company to grow and become strong and earn more money. In addition to cash, your factor provides several services which benefit your business. Likewise, as you earn more and factor more receivables, your factor's income increases with yours. It is a mutually beneficial relationship.

Unfortunately, some factoring relationships can turn sour when payments aren't forthcoming due to disputed invoices, unsatisfactory products or services rendered to customers, or customer insolvency. When these happen, cooperation with the factor is critical. The worst thing a business owner can do is consider this the factor's problem and become hard to find or uncooperative. The factor has advanced funds in good faith and is owed money. The business owner is not only legally but morally obliged to help arrive at a satisfactory resolution.

With these faulty assumptions corrected and mistakes properly avoided, we now move on to the task of determining if factoring will help your business.

Part 3

Research

Factoring: Sell Your Invoices Today, Get Cash Tomorrow

6

Is Factoring for You?

Earlier in this book, the question was posed: "If my company had all the cash on hand it needed, what would I do with that cash?" Put another way, "If my company had unlimited cash, what would this cash enable my business to do that it can't do now?" Let me break these questions down to more specific terms and encourage you to write down your answers.

Visualize the Changes in Your Business

Imagine for a moment that having adequate cash on hand was a normal way of operating your business on a daily basis...not just a wistful dream. Picture yourself receiving an infusion of cash as you sell your first batch of invoices, and continuing to do so in the coming weeks and months. By waiting a day or two instead of a month or two to be paid, you now have plenty of cash on hand...probably more than your company has ever had before.

Jot down your answers to the questions that follow in the Factoring Analysis Form.

Factoring Analysis Form

1. Which of my present customers would be beneficial to factor, and how much immediate cash could I expect from factoring their invoices?

Customer: _____

Invoice amt range: $_____ to $_____

Avg. invoice amt: $_____   Avg. mo. vol: $_____

Customer: _____

Invoice amt range: $_____ to $_____

Avg. invoice amt: $_____   Avg. mo. vol: $_____

Customer: _____

Invoice amt range: $_____ to $_____

Avg. invoice amt: $_____   Avg. mo. vol: $_____

Customer: _____

Invoice amt range: $_____ to $_____

Avg. invoice amt: $_____   Avg. mo. vol: $_____

Customer: _____

Invoice amt range: $_____ to $_____

Avg. invoice amt: $_____   Avg. mo. vol: $_____

Customer: _____

Invoice amt range: $_____ to $_____

Avg. invoice amt: $_____   Avg. mo. vol: $_____

Customer: _____

Invoice amt range: $_____ to $_____

Avg. invoice amt: $_____   Avg. mo. vol: $_____

Total Current Customers Avg. Mo. Vol.: $_____

70% Advance of Average Monthly Volume: $_____
80% Advance of Average Monthly Volume: $_____
90% Advance of Average Monthly Volume: $_____

2. By providing net 30 day terms, being able to accept new and/or larger orders, having more inventory, and/or hiring more sales staff, how much new business could I add and factor?

New Customer: _____
Invoice amt range: $_____ to $_____
Avg. invoice amt: $_____   Avg. mo. vol: $_____

New Customer: _____
Invoice amt range: $_____ to $_____
Avg. invoice amt: $_____   Avg. mo. vol: $_____

New Customer: _____
Invoice amt range: $_____ to $_____
Avg. invoice amt: $_____   Avg. mo. vol: $_____

New Customer:_____
Invoice amt range: $_____ to $_____
Avg. invoice amt: $_____   Avg. mo. vol: $_____

New Customer: _____
Invoice amt range: $_____ to $_____
Avg. invoice amt: $_____   Avg. mo. vol: $_____

New Customer: _____
Invoice amt range: $_____ to $_____
Avg. invoice amt: $_____   Avg. mo. vol: $_____

Total New Customers Avg. Mo. Vol.: | $ |

70% Advance of Average Monthly Volume: $_____
80% Advance of Average Monthly Volume: $_____
90% Advance of Average Monthly Volume: $_____

Combined Current and New Customer Total Avg. Mo. Vol.:
| $ |

Advance on Combined Total Average Monthly Volume:
   70% Advance of Average Monthly Volume: $_____
   80% Advance of Average Monthly Volume: $_____
   90% Advance of Average Monthly Volume: $_____

3. What are the first three uses I will make of this cash?

1. _____

2. _____

3. _____

4. If they are not already mentioned, what specific bills or obligations will I pay?

1. _____

2. _____

3. _____

5. What specific expenditures will I make to increase sales?

1. _____

2. _____

3. _____

6. What specific measures will I take to decrease future expenses?

1. _____

2. _____

3. _____

7. Meeting payroll on a regular basis is a common use of factored funds. What effect on my company, or what emotions will I feel (e.g. relief, less stress, less worry), by meeting payroll with adequate cash?

1. _____

2. _____

3. _____

8. A year from now, my company will be different in the following ways because I have good, steady, and dependable cash flow:

1. _____

2. _____

3. _____

====================

Once this form completed, you may decide factoring makes sense for your business. If so, create a simple spreadsheet of a "Before and After Factoring" Income Statement, similar to the one in Chapter 2. This exercise gives a further indication of the value factoring will have for your business.

Armed with the numbers you now have, the next steps are finding a factor; or, if you already are in discussions with a factor or broker, knowing what to ask and determining if a factor is suitable for you business.

7

How to Find a Factor

If you are looking for a factor on your own and don't know where to start, there are two ways to find the best factor to fund your company's receivables.

1. You can use the services of a professional factoring broker who knows the business and has contacts with a wide variety of factors.

2. You can find a factor on your own.

However, if you are already working with a broker or factor who gave you this book, chances are high you are working with a seasoned professional and you really don't need to read this chapter. In this case, save yourself a lot of time and effort, look no further, and go with the person you have; you are in good hands. Otherwise, read on.

Using a Broker

Some business owners are a bit reluctant to use a broker because they assume doing so will be an added expense. They reason that if they take the time to find a factor themselves, they will save the money a broker would cost.

However, very few brokers are paid by factoring clients. A small number may require a deposit or up-front fee to initiate their service, but most have no such requirements. A broker's income is based on commissions he receives from the factor for bringing new clients.

These commissions are usually a percentage of the discount the factor receives over the course of the factoring relationship, and come out the of the factor's pocket, not yours.

Factoring discounts you pay will typically be the same whether you're introduced to the factor by a broker or find the factor on your own, so you do not pay more to use a broker's service. A good broker will be familiar with rates various factors charge, and should serve your interest by introducing you to the one with the best rates who is most suited to your needs, thereby saving you money. Independent brokers are the sales force of the factors who use them, and they usually cost the factor less than salaried sales people.

As you can see, a skilled broker with good contacts and excellent marketing skills is valuable to both the factor and the business owner needing funds. For the factor, an able broker will screen clients who are incompatible and introduce only prospects who meet the factor's criteria. This saves the factor a great deal of time and resources in booking new business. A phone call from a good broker who has brought valuable business in the past is always a welcome event to any factor, and will be greeted with exceptional interest.

For the business owner seeking a factor, a talented broker will match you with the factor best suited to your particular business and needs. The broker's knowledge and contacts can save you countless hours of what could prove to be a time consuming and frustrating search, particularly if you are new to factoring and have no idea where to look or what to look for. And because the *factor* pays the broker, there are usually no out of pocket expenses for you.

Thus, finding and using the services of a capable broker is often the first step to a profitable factoring relationship.

Where to Look

If you need to find a broker or a factor on your own the two simplest ways are to seek a referral from people you know or look online.

Referrals

By asking associates who own a business in your industry or a similar one, you may find someone who is currently factoring or has factored invoices in the past. Obviously the advantage of this method is that if you find such a person, you can ask about his level of satisfaction with the factor used.

You can also ask for referrals from people in financial circles. If you've been turned down for a bank loan, the lending officer may have contacts with a broker or factor in the area. These are often good referrals because these people have made a point of developing a relationship with the banker, which indicates a professional marketing effort.

Occasionally you may find an accountant, bookkeeper, or financial planner who can provide a referral. However, as mentioned earlier, some financial professionals are not as familiar with factoring as you might expect, and/or may harbor negative stereotypes of the factoring industry and be reluctant to suggest someone. In this case, their ignorance or attitude will not help your search for needed capital, so keep looking.

Some factors and brokers are involved in the Chamber of Commerce or local networking/leads groups such as Business Networking International (BNI) or LeTip. Many communities have independent networking groups like these as well. Contacting such organizations may lead you to the right person who will be able to help you.

Online

Most factors and brokers have a web site which gives detailed information about their companies and the types of clients they serve.

Anyone who knows how to use a search engine like Google or Bing can look up "factoring company" or something similar. Doing so will provide an inexhaustible list that will include literally thousands of factors and go on for hundreds of pages. You then need to plod through each one, scanning their web sites to see if their service matches your company in terms of industry, dollar volume, location, and a host of other characteristics.

You'll quickly be overwhelmed with such a general search. So narrow your keywords to those that describe your business. For example, if you are a very small company look up "small business factoring. If you make furniture, look up "factor for furniture manufacturing." Narrow the search by adding your city, state, or region. You'll still need to plow through pages of listings, but the hits should be more specific to what you're looking for.

Sites with Lists of Factors

You may come upon sites that provide lists of factors, or data base matching services with factoring companies. Sites that provide simple lists usually sort the factors by state, and/or by the name of the factoring company, and occasionally by client business size or niche. Those sorted by state are helpful when you want to find a factor in your region. Those sorted by name are helpful if you already know the name of the factor you want, perhaps from a referral, but you have no contact information. Those sorted by niche obviously help you weed out those who do not service your industry or the size of your company. Remember that none of these lists or matching sites can include every single factor out there. Also, new sites like these can appear any time while others may disappear.

If you do internet searches you will likely come upon exchange sites such as The Receivables Exchange, Receivables-market.com, and QuarterSpot. These sites have appeared as internet technology has developed and are relatively new compared to traditional factoring.

The advantages of these sites are:

1. You can spot factor a single invoice or two fairly easily.

2. Your costs and discount rates may (or may not) be lower.

3. You usually aren't making a long-term commitment to a particular factor.

Disadvantages of these sites are:

1. You are working with the exchange instead of the funder, and if you need a long-term factor you are probably better off finding and working with one directly.

2. Your costs and discount rates may (or may not) be higher. Do your homework.

3. There have been a few legal issues with at least one of these sites that would probably have not developed with clients working directly with a funder.

While these sites offer an interesting alternative to traditional factoring, regular factoring companies will continue to serve businesses across the country as long as businesses need money.

+   +   +

One final word about finding a factor. Some people assume that flooding numerous potential factors with notice of your desire for factoring will lead to the most number of inquiries about your company. Actually, the opposite may result.

The best plan is *not* to get as many possible "feelers" out there, but to be methodical and plan your strategy. In other words, if you decide to use a broker, work with only one broker at a time and let the broker do her job. Don't tell the broker to find a factor for you, then use another broker without telling the first broker. And don't continue to look yourself in addition to having the broker look for you. Why?

Chances are high that a factor will learn what you're doing because your account will be presented from more than one source. This tells the factor that you're "shopping" your deal which is a quick turn-off if you don't tell the factor this right from the start. Because factors put a good deal of time and usually expense into researching new prospects, the appearance that other factors are doing the same will incline most to lose interest quickly. The factor's reasoning is simply this: "I don't want to go to the effort and expense of considering this prospect if six other factors are doing the same thing, which considerably lessens my chance of closing this deal."

Factors who participate in bidding sites expect the stiffer competition, but those who don't use these sites choose not to do business this way. If your deal comes to them from two or three brokers, or a broker and one or two web sites, it's clear your deal is being shopped and the interest in your account will disappear quickly – not just from one factor, but from most or all of them. Therefore, pick one strategy and stay with it.

If after a reasonable time frame your broker hasn't found a factor, or you haven't been able to find a factor from one particular web site, try another. Just give each one a fair chance before moving on.

If your business is indeed factorable and you utilize the variety of resources described in this chapter, you should be able to find *at least* one factor suitable to your needs who will work with you!

Now that you have direction as to how to find a factor, we turn to what to look for in a factor. As you will see, you need to look for a great deal more than price alone.

8
What to Look for in a Factor

Features

Now that you've determined factoring your company's receivables is both possible and beneficial and know how to find a factor, there are many features in a factor to consider. These features include the niche or niches a factor serves, factoring dollar volume required, services provided, and more. Let's take a look at each of these features to help you determine if a certain factor is suitable for your company's needs.

Niches Served

Like most businesses, factoring companies serve various niche markets. These can be defined by size of clients funded and/or specific industries served.

For example, one industry niche is medical receivables. Purchasing the receivables of medical clinics, physicians, and others who bill insurance companies and/or Medicare is a specialized factoring niche which requires specific expertise on the factor's part. Most factors don't provide medical receivables factoring; conversely, those who specialize in medical receivables often do not factor "standard" receivables. A few larger factors who provide standard factoring might have an arm of their company that services the medical clients. However, factors who fund the standard manufacturing, sales and service industries usually do not purchase medical receivables.

Other factors may focus on certain industry niches such as trucking, nurse staffing, or office staffing, but serve other unrelated client industries as well.

Size of the clients funded is another niche that enables business owners to determine which factors fund businesses of their size. Let's look at this more closely.

Volume Required

Larger factors will serve larger business clients whose minimum volume is $100,000 and goes to millions in factored invoices each month. Very small factors may go to the opposite extreme and fund only businesses whose monthly factoring volume is less than $10,000 or $20,000 per month. The majority of factors fall somewhere in between and most have minimum factoring volumes of $25,000 or $50,000 per month.

Some mid-range factors will claim to have no minimum monthly volume requirements. However, their profit threshold is usually funding clients who factor $25,000 to $50,000 per month. They might say they accept the under $10,000 clients, but in fact don't really welcome them, especially if there are no indications of future growth that will come quickly.

Very small businesses with low sales volume who need factoring should seek out factors who serve the niche of very small clients. These small niche factors specialize in very small accounts and *prefer* the clients whose factoring volume is under $10,000 per month. For some time these small factors were few in number, but their ranks are steadily increasing.

When you discuss with a factor the niche he serves, don't try to make your business conform to that niche if in fact it doesn't. For example, if your business is really only going to be able to factor $10,000 per month and the factor states his monthly minimum requirements are $25,000, don't artificially inflate the volume of which your company is capable in an effort to interest this factor in funding you. You're better served to find a factor who prefers to work with a company your size.

Likewise, if you're a trucking company and you find a factor who prefers not to fund trucking receivables, don't try to talk him into accepting your account. Keep looking. There are many factors who welcome trucking receivables; in fact many specialize in the niche of transportation factoring.

Services Provided

While factoring is a business whose focus is financing, it is especially a service business. Factors provide their clients numerous services and you want to be clear what a factor can do for you before you get under way. If a factor simply funds your receivables and nothing more, you may be missing out on some of the most important services available. So besides cash for your invoices, what services do factors provide?

Credit Screening

It behooves both you and the factor to know the creditworthiness of your customers. When you become a client, a factor will run a credit check on the customers whose invoices you wish to sell to determine if they are a good credit risk. This can be done quickly and easily by the factor's use of one of several credit bureaus. The factor simply pulls a credit report, obtains the credit rating, and accepts or rejects a customer based on what's found.

Once your factoring relationship is under way and you want to factor new customers, your factor will run a credit check to determine the new customer's creditworthiness. This is a great benefit to you, because learning a new customer's credit standing will help you determine if you want to (and will be able to) factor the customer, require COD terms, or simply not do business with him in the first place. This service alone is one of the greatest benefits to your business, especially a new or small one, who has not utilized credit information before. Credit screening can save you from financial losses and untold headaches due to deadbeat customers, whom you otherwise just assumed would pay you.

Quality Control

To limit their risk, factors routinely seek some type of verification from your customers that your invoices are valid and will

79

be paid in a timely fashion. This serves as an added layer of quality control for your business.

When you submit new invoices and a factor verifies them with a phone call, faxed letter, or other sign-off from your customer, this provides assurance that your customer is happy with your product or service and will pay in a timely fashion. This in turn minimizes the number of disputed invoices you experience and assures both you and the factor of the soundness of your receivables. It also indicates to your customer that you care about the quality of your product or service and take an extra measure to make sure they are satisfied.

Billing

Some (though not all) factors are equipped to take over your billing if this will benefit you. Consider how much time and money you or your employees spend creating invoices, preparing them for mailing, and sending them. If you can outsource this task to your factor, how much will that save you in time and money?

If little of the factor's time is involved, those who provide this service may do so for minimal cost. If considerable time is required, the cost may still be less than you're presently spending for these tasks. On the other hand, if you prefer to continue to do your own billing, this is usually fine with most factors.

Delinquent Accounts Contact

One of the biggest chores for many small businesses is contacting customers whose payments are past due. Such collection efforts are usually a routine part of a factor's service. Having your factor determine the payment status of your overdue invoice payments relieves a great burden from many business owners and their staffs.

Most factors' account managers watch clients' aging reports closely and make needed follow-up calls as part of their daily work. When handled professionally, this keeps the number of delinquent payments much lower than it would be if neglected because the business owner or bookkeeper is too busy to do it.

Some business owners prefer to maintain contact with their customers who are slow to pay. While some factors prefer to take responsibility for such contacts, others either allow you to make these calls or work together with you to collect slow paying accounts.

When you are considering using a factor's services, ask about his policy for handling delinquent payments and be sure you are comfortable with the answer. If not, determine how flexible the factor is in this regard. If you are left with the sense that you don't want your customers to be handled by this factor's methods, look for another factor.

Notification and Non-Notification

In order to limit the risk of not receiving payments for factored invoices, factors ordinarily require that customers send payments to an address controlled by the factor. This can be their office, post office box, or a lock box. If paid by direct deposit, funds must go directly to the factor's bank account. This means your customers need to be informed of this change of address or banking information for their remittances.

Most factors will require that checks be made out in the factor's name. Some will want the factor's name, followed by "FBO ABC Company," where "ABC Company" is the client's business name. "FBO" means "For Benefit Of," and enables everyone to know whose invoices are being paid if there is a question. Still other factors allow the checks to be made out to the client's company name, but require payment be sent to the factor's remittance address.

Occasionally business owners factoring their receivables will not want their customers to be aware a factoring relationship exists. They will demand "non-notification" factoring whereby the customer is not informed the business is factoring. This may make the verification of invoices a little more tricky than in a "notification" relationship, and requires the checks continue to be made out to the client's business. Some factors are not willing to work on a strict non-notification basis because it means more work and less security for them. Consequently, those who offer this usually charge more for it. However, in most cases non-notification is really not needed in the first place and you're better off working on a notification basis.

If you think non-notification is an absolute requirement for you, ask a prospective factor if he will work on this basis, and to describe how his company maintains the level of secrecy from your customers that is needed.

In any event, very few factors will allow payments to routinely come to an address the factor does not control. It's simply too easy for a client to "accidentally" bank a factored payment or "forget" to give a factored payment check to the factor. As we have seen, these actions constitute fraud and are taken very seriously by factors and their attorneys.

Reports Provided

Communication from your factor, especially in regard to the status of your customers' payments, is critical. Be sure your factor will provide you timely and regular updates as to the status of your account.

This can be done through factoring reports that are printed, faxed, emailed, or (best of all) made available on the internet. Online factoring software that provides internet reporting is available to factors of all sizes, and is far preferable to you than having to wait for your factor to generate and send updated reports – which are quickly outdated shortly after you receive them. Online reports are available 24/7 and the data is updated in real time.

Any factor should be able to track your account and let you know updated information, one way or another. At the very least you should be able to know which invoices have paid, which remain outstanding, for how long they have been outstanding, and how much your discounts are to date.

Again, ask ahead of time how information is provided so you can be aware of the status of your account. Also ask to see a sample report or a demonstration of how to access your information online if that's available. Be sure you understand what you see; if the reports are too complicated to understand, instant access to them means nothing.

Response Time

Funding Time Frames

Because you're factoring to improve your cash flow a key question is, "How long will I wait to receive the advance after submitting my invoices?" Depending on the size of your account and the size of your factor, setting up a new account usually takes anywhere from a few days to a couple weeks. Medical receivables can take a month or two. Once your account is set up and you have received your first funding, future advances happen quickly. Most factors provide advances within 48 hours of invoice submission; many promise 24 hour turnaround, and in some cases factors can provide same day funding.

Just as important, be sure you understand clearly a factor's method and timing of providing rebates once an invoice pays. Some factors will put a portion of your rebate in a reserve account which will act as a buffer against future uncollected or short payments.

Some factors will pay rebates only after all the invoices in a batch are paid. Others pay rebates once a month, others pay weekly, some pay after a customer's check clears, and a few pay the next business day after receiving payment. There is a fairly wide variety of practices here, so be sure you understand and are comfortable with your prospective factor's practice in this regard.

Response Time to Inquiries

You will be working closely with your factor and from time to time will have a question, need a report, or some other piece of information. Will your account executive be dependably available during business hours? How heavy is this person's case load and how quickly will your call be answered or returned? Once your question is asked, how much time will pass before you receive the report or answer?

Location

There are advantages to working with a factor in your area, though for most people this is not a requirement. You can maintain face-to-face contact, drop by the office, and generally get to know first-hand the people who are servicing your account. They will also share an understanding of the local economic and social conditions in which your business operates.

On the other hand, you may not be able to locate a factor in your area who meets your particular needs. If you need a niche factor, you may have no choice but to work with one located elsewhere. Fortunately dealing with a factor in a different part of the country can be done quite efficiently, and a large percentage of many factors' clients are located in distant parts of the country.

Recourse and Nonrecourse Factoring

Most smaller and medium-sized factors operate on a recourse basis. That means if your customer does not pay for any reason after a specified number of days, your company must repay the factor for the advance given and discount earned. This can be done in a number of ways, including exchanging a new invoice for the unpaid one, deducting the amount owed from advances and/or rebates from other invoices that have paid or will pay, deducting funds from reserves held, or outright payments of cash.

The need to make good on unpaid invoices makes clear the reason to factor only good-paying customers, and why determining a customer's creditworthiness is important for both you and the factor. Remember, factors are not collection companies to whom you sell poor-paying accounts; they are financing companies who are in business to purchase good receivables.

Some medium-sized and larger factors work on a non-recourse basis, which means if your customers do not pay due to insolvency or bankruptcy, the factor will absorb the loss. This amounts to credit insurance for businesses who work with non-recourse factors and is an added benefit to the factoring relationship.

However you must appreciate the fact that non-recourse factors will naturally be particularly careful about the invoices they purchase. If there is any indication a customer will not pay, non-recourse factors are quick to exclude these accounts from those they purchase. What's more, if a customer does not pay an invoice because of a dispute, the non-recourse nature of the agreement is not in effect. If your customer refuses to pay because he says an invoice is inaccurate or because products or services were defective, the factor still has recourse to you.

Most non-recourse factors make the non-recourse aspect of their service clear in their marketing materials. This does not necessarily make their company more suited to yours, as they could decline your customers as too risky. Generally speaking, non-recourse is a desirable feature but not necessarily the only reason to choose one factor over another. Just be sure you understand what will happen in the event of non-payment. Whether your factor operates on a recourse or non-recourse basis, only sell invoices which you are confident will pay in a timely manner.

Capitalization

When looking for a factor, a reasonable question to ask (but often overlooked by many business owners) is the source and adequacy of a factor's capital. Medium to large factors are usually financed with sizeable bank lines, and are quite capable of financing a number of large accounts. However, you should know what would happen to your account if your factor's bank line were called (required to be repaid immediately), and the circumstances and likelihood of that happening in the first place.

Much smaller factors are typically capitalized with personal funds from the owner, and/or private funds, and/or loans and lines from banks or companies who fund factors. In general the more diverse the sources of a small factor's capitalization, or the more the funds come from the small factor's personal funds, the more stable that factor's capitalization will be. If any factor, no matter how large or small, obtains his or her funds from a single outside source that can be pulled with short or no notice, that factor's operation may need to make fast and perhaps unexpected adjustments. You want to work with a factor whose source of funds are as stable and as much in the factor's control as possible.

Application and Setup Fees

In general, the larger the clients a factor serves, the larger the application and setup fees tend to be. Some industry niches, medical factoring in particular, tend to have very high due diligence fees because the time and cost of approving a client is quite extensive. With medical factoring, a complete audit of a clinic's or practice's billing and receivables is required, which can take a month or more and cost the factor several thousand dollars. At least part, and often all, of this cost is usually required of the prospective client.

Factors who fund standard receivables do not have the extensive requirements of medical factors, but they do have due diligence expenses when examining a prospective client and her customers. A factor will usually run background checks to determine the existence of anything that could impact the factor's collateral, such as existing personal or business liens, tax liens, judgments, criminal history, and the like. These costs come out of the factor's pocket before any discounts are earned on new accounts. Therefore, many factors charge a fee to cover these costs and call it an application fee, setup fee, due diligence fee, or another similar name.

Many factors use this application fee to separate the "tire kickers" from prospective clients who are serious about factoring. Spending several hundred dollars on due diligence for a prospect who turns out to be "just looking" is not good business for any factor, and justifies charging this fee. Some factors are more flexible about these fees and may reimburse some or all of these costs after a client has been factoring long enough to cover them. Still others consider their due diligence expenses to be the cost of doing business and charge little or nothing for setup fees.

For exceptionally small factors, several hundred dollars in application fees can simply be more than their very small prospective clients can afford; therefore some very small factors charge low or no setup fees. Because the amounts that will be funded are substantially less than those for larger factors, smaller factors may be somewhat less thorough in their due diligence procedures, and therefore pay less for them. In turn, their due diligence fees may be lower or non-existent.

Application fees are certainly worth asking about and you should be clear as to the due diligence searches on which these funds are spent. By not balking at the payment of an application fee, if it seems to be a reasonable amount, you are showing a prospective factor that you are serious about doing business. But if you appear to be trying to weasel out of this legitimate expense, many factors will understandably lose interest in working with you.

Advance and Discount Rates

"How much do you advance?" and "How much will it cost me?" are the two most common questions any business owner will ask a prospective factor. The answers will vary drastically depending on numerous issues related to your industry, your customers, and your own business circumstances.

In general, the higher the risk posed by your receivables, the lower your advance and the higher your discounts. Over the past several years, there has been a gradual and slight increase in standard advances and a lowering of discounts. This has been caused by more competition among factors for existing business, as these rates are somewhat driven by what the market will bear. Therefore, stating specific advances or discounts here can be somewhat misleading, as they can change with economic conditions. Some general observations will help, however.

Those in industries where the risk of nonpayment is higher will generally expect to receive lower advances. Those who wish to factor construction receivables may find few factors willing to purchase them. Those who do fund construction invoices provide lower advances, often around 50% to 70%, for receivables they will purchase...and even then, construction factors will have very specific requirements for the invoices they buy. If these are not strictly met, the invoices will be declined.

Likewise, medical receivables paid by insurance companies and Medicare may receive lower advances because the amount insurance companies pay for medical billings is erratic and less than the amount of a bill. This can result in advances as low as 25% to 70% of the amount of expected payout, rather than a percentage of the value of the invoice.

At present, those in industries with invoices to dependably paying customers whose total monthly volume is quite low can expect advances to typically be in the 70% to 80% range. A few factors funding very small businesses may advance more, but will sometimes charge high flat discounts in return.

For example, a typical small factor specializing in small businesses might advance 75% and charge 5% or 6% for the first 30 days an invoice is outstanding, and an additional 1% for each week thereafter. A larger factor who accepts small clients (which most don't) might give a 90% advance, but charge a flat discount of 10%, no matter how long an invoice is outstanding. However, such factors may not accept customers who take over 45 days to pay. So while the advance they provide is high, the discounts are high as well. In this scenario, the client is usually better off to use the smaller factor with the lower advance because the discounts will be lower. Further, a small factor is usually able to offer more personalized service than a larger factor, and overall is simply better suited to the needs of a very small client.

As a business' dollar volume of factoring increases, advances tend to increase and discounts decrease. Clients who have good paying customers who factor between $25,000 to $100,000 per month can expect to receive advances ranging between 70% to 90%, and occasionally slightly more. Don't automatically expect to receive the higher end of these advances; these are simply broad ranges that are usually offered. Your industry, the creditworthiness of your customers, the stability of your own business, and the return on investment a factor needs to make will determine what is offered. While some factors allow room for negotiation with their terms, don't expect to negotiate drastic changes, and in some cases there may be no room for negotiation at all.

Discounts can be calculated in a dizzying number of combinations. Many factors have a beginning discount for the first 7, 10, 15 or 30 days. After this, discounts increase based on incremental periods which can be the next 15, 10, 7, or 1 day/s. The additional rates for each of these incremental periods will vary also, but generally will reflect the initial 15 or 30 day period. That is, if the first 30 days cost 4%, the next 7 to 10 days might be an additional 1%. The larger the invoice volume, the smaller these discounts tend to be and the smaller the initial and following incremental periods.

Be sure you understand how advances and discounts are calculated. Advances are usually a percentage of the face value of the invoice. Be sure to ask if this is true with a prospective factor; if it's not, be clear how an advance amount is derived.

Discounts – what you pay the factor – are a percentage of the invoice amount rather than the advance amount. This is because, by definition, the factor buys an invoice "at a discount" of the invoice's face value. Loan interest is based on the loan amount. Factoring is not a loan and based on how much an invoice is discounted.

Discounts are usually calculated based on the period of time which begins when the advance is given and ends when the factor receives payment. There can be exceptions to this, however. For example, some factors start the clock on the date of the invoice, rather than the date of the advance. Others will stop the clock a certain number of days after the payment is received by the factor, which gives time for the check to clear. Again, be sure you know how your factor makes these important calculations and that this information is clearly stated in your contractual documents.

Advances and discounts are the most carefully considered features of a factor's proposal to prospective clients, so be sure you understand what is offered and carefully do the math to make sure it works for you. A good factor will want to work out an arrangement that is win-win for both of you, so be sure you feel this is the case before you commit to a working relationship.

Other Charges – Hidden and Stated

There are break-even points for any factoring company, and income thresholds below which a factor cannot profitably operate. Therefore those who offer exceptionally low factoring rates compared to others may include other charges that don't immediately meet the eye. Be sure you get a clear indication from the very beginning of all discounts and charges you will pay.

For example, Factor A is willing to purchase a client's monthly receivables which total $95,000 per month for 3% for the first 30 days, and .1% calculated on a daily basis after that, and provide an 85% advance. Factor B will also give an 85% advance, but charges only 1% for the first 30 plus a similar follow-up discount after that.

Why such a difference? Factor B also charges a flat "transaction fee" of 1.5% of every factored transaction in addition to "customary" discounts such as Factor A disclosed. This wasn't stated in the preliminary presentation to the client, who naturally was inclined to go with Factor B...until this item came to light. Therefore, be sure you carefully read the contract and insist on a clear statement in writing of every discount and fee that will be charged.

If a factor wires funds to your bank account or overnights a check, you will be charged for this, usually anywhere from $15 to $30. If funds are wired, be aware that your bank will also charge you to receive the wire transfer. Again, be sure you know ahead of time what the fees are.

Monthly Minimums and Term Contracts

Some factors proudly state they have no monthly minimums nor long term contracts. What does that mean? In order to make an adequate profit, especially when a client's volume is small or somewhat marginal, some factors will require monthly minimum volumes and that clients factor for a stated length of time. This guarantees the factor the level of income needed for profitability.

For example, a factor might require a minimum factoring volume of $10,000 per month for 12 consecutive months. That means the client must pay a minimum factoring charge, regardless of the dollar volume of invoices he factors, every month for 12 months. If the monthly minimum charge is $1,000 and the client has a seasonal business with no invoices to factor over the summer, the $1,000 must still be paid during each of those months.

Contracts that require you factor for a stated period of time, usually 12 to 24 months, can be difficult to leave if you feel the need. For example, perhaps your business volume has decreased since you started factoring and meeting the monthly minimum has become difficult; continuing to reach it for the remaining term of the contract will be even more of a challenge.

If you tell your factor you want to stop factoring or go to another factor (who doesn't have monthly minimums or a term contract), your present factor may cooperate and let you go since he's not making enough from your account to be profitable. However, not all factors will be so cooperative, and yours might hold you to the time remaining on your contract. In other words, she may not agree to let you go, or may charge a steep penalty for doing so which typically makes leaving financially unviable. Again, read your contract carefully for such requirements and penalties so you know clearly what your contractual responsibilities are. Expect your factor to enforce them.

Obviously it is to your advantage to find a factor who will have no minimums or long-term requirements. These terms are often employed by larger factors who accept small clients, and are used to ensure the factor's overhead costs are met to service this small account. When a business owner is looking for a factor, this is an important question to raise. Chances are good you will find a factor suited to your size business who will not have this requirement.

Consider More Than Just a Factor's Advances and Discounts

When looking for a factor, just like looking for any other service or product, the first thing most people consider is price. We all want the best deal for the lowest cost, whether we're buying a car, shopping for clothes, or looking for a factor. But just like any other search for the best deal, price is only one part of the equation. People who make a decision based solely on the lowest cost often come to regret their decision to "go cheap." As we all know, you usually get what you pay for.

But that's not to say you should choose a factor with the highest price, either; that can be as bad a decision as buying a Cadillac when you need a Chevy. As we'll see in the next chapter, there are many considerations you need to weigh when choosing a factor.

For example, maybe a higher advance is more important to you than paying a low discount. Or perhaps a lower discount means more to you than a higher advance. Another person may look for a factor with top notch support. Capable, professional staff who service his account with consistent, friendly efficiency are more important to him than the advance or discount amounts. Someone else may want a factor experienced in her particular industry. Yet another business owner may want to work with a factor he can see face to face and thus wants a local factor.

In short, determine what is most important to you. Remember: making your choice based *only* on price can be a bad decision. You need the confidence not just that you're getting a reasonable deal, you also need the assurance you're in good hands.

Look at it this way. If you had a rare disease, would you want to go to the doctor or clinic who knows how to treat what you have, or would you go to the provider who charges the lowest fee? Which is more important, your health or the cost to maintain it? While those with poor or no insurance may not have a good choice here, we all want the best treatment we can get. Consider factoring the same way – after all, you're dealing with the health of your company.

Now that you have a better idea of what to look for in a factor, we turn to making contact with a factor and asking the right questions to determine that a) you fit the factor's parameters, and b) the factor provides the services you seek.

9

What to Ask
a Factor

Determining a Factor's Suitability
for Your Business

Through your broker or your own efforts you have now located a prospective factor to purchase your receivables. You want to be sure you meet the factor's requirements and the factor is suitable to your needs, as well.

When first speaking to a business development officer or principal of a factoring company, there are several items you need to tell her before you determine this factor's suitability for your needs. Paint a brief but complete picture of your business so the factor will know whether you fit the parameters of companies she funds. With full disclosure on your part, the fact that you don't meet her requirements may become apparent quickly. Don't fret over this; if you truly have a factorable business, you're simply one step closer to finding the right factor. If this person can't help you, ask for a referral if you or your broker don't have other factors to contact.

Below is a Factor Consultation Form you can use to quickly determine if you and a factor are compatible. You may not want to discuss every single item here, but covering many or most of these bases will show that you are serious –and informed – about factoring. Most potential clients tend to take "pot luck" in factors, so garnering this information will help you make an educated decision when you decide on a factor. What's more, the knowledge you show by asking these questions will pique the factor's interest in working with you; she'll see you're doing your homework and will respect you as a sharp and savvy businessperson. Such people make desirable clients for factors.

Further, both of you will save time if this isn't the right match. Many factoring deals are killed at the last minute, often after a great deal of time and expense, when a piece of information is learned that could and should have been stated at the beginning. If this killer information had been disclosed early, the deal would not have moved forward and no time would have been wasted by anyone. Full disclosure is in your interest as well as the factor's.

Once you have described your company and your factoring needs (Part 1 below) and your company seems to fit the factor's parameters, you want to learn of the factor's requirements, services, and charges (Part 2).

You may wish to fill out Part 1 prior to your call. You can then make contact, describe your business in a concise and methodical way that includes what the factor needs to know, and proceed with the conversation. Being organized this way will save both you and the factor time, and increase the factor's interest in working with you.

Factor Consultation Form

PART 1

1. Describe your company to the factor:
    a. Industry: _____

    b. Organized as a: __Corporation __LLC

                         __Partnership   __ □Sole Proprietor

    c. Length of time in business: _____

    d. Owner's experience: _____

    e. Approximate monthly factoring volume:

                        $_____

    f. Approximate number of invoices to factor monthly:

                 _____

    g. Average invoice size: $_____

    h. Typical range of invoice size: $_____

                      to $_____

    i. Number of customers to factor: _____

    j. Industries and/or names of a few customers:

            _____

            _____

    k. Customers' payment history and/or credit rating:

            _____

            _____

    l. Specific reasons you wish to factor:

        __ Meet Payroll   __ Purchase Equipment

        __ Pay Bills   __ Increase Staff

        __ Pay Taxes   __ Obtain Cash Discounts

        __ Other: _____

2. Disclose any of the following:
    ___ Existing bank loans/lines of credit

    ___ UCC liens and assets they secure

    ___ Taxes in arrears and/or tax liens

    ___ Judgments against you or your company

    ___ Pending litigation in which you are a defendant

    ___ Bankruptcies, past or present

PART 2

Factor: _____

Contact: _____

Phone: _____

Location: _____

Web Site: _____

Email: _____

Opening Questions

1. Do you fund companies in my industry? ___ Yes ___ No

2. What are your clients' monthly factoring volumes:
   Preferred Range: $_____ to $_____
   Minimum: $_____
   Maximum: $_____

3. What are your typical advances and discounts for businesses in my industry with customers similar to mine?
   Advances   _____%
   Discounts   _____% for first _____ days
   Thereafter: _____

   _____

   _____

Operations and Procedures

Application

1. Typical time to set up a new account: _____

2. Turnaround time to receive advances: _____

Requirements

1. Do you require factoring for a specific length of time (term contracts)? ___ Yes ___ No
   If yes, what is the length of time? _____

2. Do you have a minimum charge per month?

___ Yes ___ No ___ Depends
If yes, what is the amount? $_____

Advances

1. What methods do you use to advance funds, and what are the charges if any?

    ___ Check pick up at your office $_____
    ___ US Mail $_____
    ___ Bank deposit $_____
    ___ Bank wire $_____
    ___ Overnight check $_____
    ___ ACH $_____
    ___ Other $_____

2. Do you keep any reserves in addition to the advance hold back?

___ Yes ___ No
If yes, please explain: _____

_____

_____

Rebates

1. How do you pay rebates?
___ Per invoice   ___ Other: _____
___ Per schedule

2. How often do you pay rebates?
    ___ Daily
    ___ Weekly
    ___ Monthly
    ___ Other: _____

3. What is your procedure for paying rebates?

_____

_____

Other Fees

1. Describe other charges in addition to your factoring discounts:
___ Application/Set up $_____

    ___ Base fee or points per transaction $_____

    ___ Credit checks $_____

    ___ Wire charges $_____

    ___ Overnight delivery charges $_____

    ___ ACH or direct deposit charges $_____

    ___ Billing/Invoicing $_____

    ___ Other $_____

2. Is the application fee refundable if you:

    decline my account? ___ Yes ___ No

    accept my account? ___ Yes ___ No

    If Yes, how is the refund made?

_____

_____

Closing Documents

1. Do you require:

    ___ Personal guarantees

    ___ Business financials

    ___ Tax returns

    ___ Business plan

    ___ Other requirements _____

_____

2. What collateral do you secure on your UCC?

    ___ Accounts Receivable

    ___ More, including:

_____

_____

Customer Credit

1. How do you obtain credit information on my customers?

_____

_____

2. What credit information will you provide me about them?

_____

_____

Customer Management

1. Describe your procedures for invoice verifications.

_____

_____

2. How I am informed of the status of my account and my customers' payments?

     ___ Internet reports   Frequency: _____

     ___ Emailed reports   Frequency: _____

     ___ Faxed reports   Frequency: _____

     ___ Other means   Frequency: _____

Where can I see some sample reports you provide?

_____

3. What are your procedures if my customer's payment is past due?

_____

_____

Staff

1. Who will manage my account on a daily basis?

_____

2. How long has he/she worked in factoring and with your company?

_____   _____

99

3. What is his/her experience with my industry?

_____

Specialties *(ask only if you require these)*
1. Do you provide non-recourse factoring?
     __ Yes __ No

2. Do you provide non-notification factoring?
     __ Yes __ No

   What are your procedures for non-notification?

   _____

   _____

3. Do you provide invoicing services? __ Yes __ No
   If Yes, is this an added charge? __ Yes __ No
                    Amount: $_____

Company Background
1. How long has your company been in operation?

2. What experience does your company have factoring my type of business?

_____

_____

3. What is the source of your company's capital?
   __ Bank/institutional funds
   __ Owner funds
   __ Private investors
   __ Public company
   __ Other _____

Other

1. Do you give referral fees if I provide you leads?
     __ Yes __ No
     If Yes, what is the amount? $_____

2. Other questions:

_____

_____

_____

_____

Notes

Part 4

Taking
the Plunge

10
Signing On

Once you have found a factor, the next step is to apply and receive approval. That accomplished, funding happens quickly.

If you have ever applied for a bank loan, you'll find the application process with factors to be much simpler and faster. Gaining approval may take only one to three days for smaller factors, a week to two weeks for larger factors, and as much as a couple months for specialized niches like medical factors. In general, expect the process to average between 3 to 10 days before your account is approved and first funding is received. Once you are approved, future advances usually take between 4 to 48 hours to process for most factors. Those who apply for bank loans often experience waits that take weeks or months, and must wait this long when applying for each new loan.

While each factor will have his own forms and requirements, there is a fair amount of consistency in the information needed, particularly among factors who are about the same size.

On the next page is a flowchart of the pre-funding process. Steps 1 through 6 have been covered in previous chapters. The rest of this chapter and the remaining chapters will describe the final steps.

Pre-Funding Flowchart

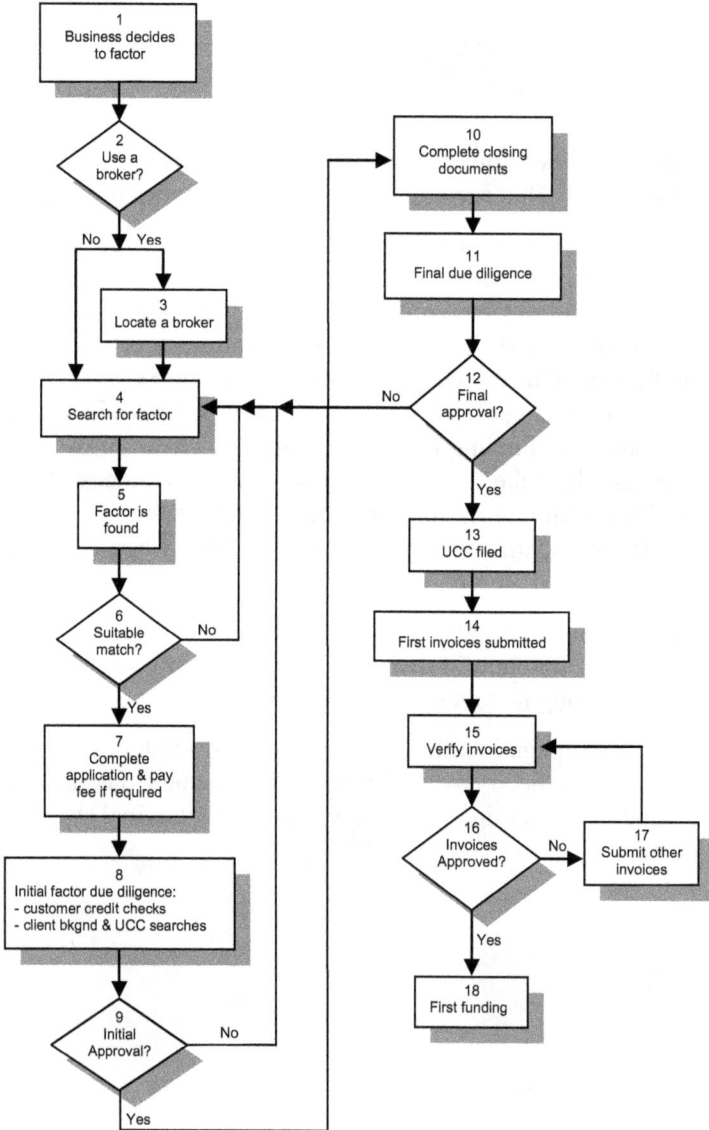

```
1
Business decides
to factor
      |
      v
2
Use a broker?
  No /     \ Yes
     |       |
     |       v
     |     3
     |   Locate a broker
     |       |
     v       v
4
Search for factor
      |
      v
5
Factor is found
      |
      v
6
Suitable match?  --- No --->
  Yes |
      v
7
Complete application & pay
fee if required
      |
      v
8
Initial factor due diligence:
- customer credit checks
- client bkgnd & UCC searches
      |
      v
9
Initial Approval?  --- No --->
  Yes |
```

```
10
Complete closing documents
      |
      v
11
Final due diligence
      |
      v
12
Final approval?  --- No ---> (to 4 Search for factor)
  Yes |
      v
13
UCC filed
      |
      v
14
First invoices submitted
      |
      v
15
Verify invoices  <---
      |              |
      v              |
16                   |
Invoices Approved?  --- No ---> 17 Submit other invoices
  Yes |
      v
18
First funding
```

The Application Process

The process begins with filling out an application form. Many factors provide this form on their web site which can be completed online.

Some will ask for more information than others, but virtually all will want the following information sooner or later. If you have used the Factor Consultation Form in the last chapter, the factor will already know much of this information.

- Company name
- Contact name and title
- Address
- Phone number
- Fax number
- Email
- Web site
- Industry
- Length of time in business
- Dollar volume to factor, usually a monthly average
- Average invoice size
- Number of customers to factor
- Names of a few customers you wish to factor
- Examples of typical invoices and an aging report
- Business type (corporation, LLC, partnership, sole proprietor)
- Federal Identification Number (which is the social security number of a sole proprietor)
- Existence of UCC liens, delinquent taxes, pending litigation, and judgments
- Existence of existing loans or lines of credit

If some of the above is not requested initially, it will probably be required later. Some factors, usually those who fund larger clients, may require the following in addition to the above:

- Annual sales
- Names and addresses of principals and/or board members of the company
- Business financials
- Tax returns
- Bank reference
- Business references
- Names of accountant and attorney

Why This Information Is Needed

The purpose of the application is to qualify prospects and eliminate those who do not fit a factor's requirements. As mentioned, factors look for particular industries, size of receivables and businesses, creditworthy customers who will be paying the invoices, and sometimes clients located within a geographic region. Everything on the application is there to indicate whether a prospect meets the factor's requirements. Let's look at each of the items and what they tell the factor.

The first seven items listed above (**Company name** through **Web site**) give demographic and contact information. Factors who fund clients in specific regions can quickly determine if a prospect meets this first requirement. The other information provides easy contact information, and if the company has a web site, will tell the factor a bit about what the business does, market niche, and customers targeted.

The next two items, **Industry** and **Length of time in business** quickly tell the factor if this is an industry they factor and the experience of those running the company. There are certain industries some factors avoid, and certain industries in which some factors specialize. Likewise, some factors prefer not to work with startup companies, while others seek them. This information further speeds up the screening process.

The next three items tell the factor if this prospect is the size of business the factor funds. **Dollar volume** will indicate if this prospect is too small, too large, or just right for the factor. Some factors also have minimum **invoice sizes** they purchase. Some factors don't want to buy individual invoices smaller than $100 or $500 or $1000, while others may prefer small invoices because they believe these minimize their risk of a substantial loss.

Like invoice size, the **Number of customers to factor** is an indication of risk and also the amount of processing time the account will require. Having only one customer means a more concentrated risk but faster processing, while numerous customers suggest well distributed risk but more time.

Naturally, the **Names of customers** to factor is one of the most important pieces of information. Usually addresses and phone numbers are requested so the factor can determine the companies' creditworthiness. Customers are not contacted at this point in the process, and the contact information is needed here only to check credit. If customers have strong credit histories, they will be valued by the factor and probably approved. If credit histories are weak or non-existent, those customers will probably be declined. If a prospective client has many customers, the stronger ones are likely to be accepted and the weaker ones refused.

Examples of typical invoices give the factor a feel for the prospect's billing procedures, which is an important aspect of the factor's work. Invoices that are hand-written, created with accounting software, or billed electronically each tell the factor helpful information as to a prospective business owner's experience, level of technical and/or bookkeeping know-how, and general business sophistication. These in turn will help the factor determine how to best work with this client, what services the factor provides that can help the client, and how much of the factor's time this will require.

An **Aging report** will give the factor extremely helpful information regarding this company's customer payment trends. This report, which can be easily generated in accounting software like QuickBooks, will list customers and the length of time they take to pay their bills. These times are usually listed in columns, such as Current, 0-30, 31-60, 61-90, and Over 90 days. Customers who are in the first three columns are the best candidates for factoring, while those who drag out longer are less desirable, both for the factor and the client. If a collection agency is needed for problem accounts, the factor can probably recommend one. A few factors have an in-house collection agency.

All the information thus far will go into the factor's calculations of what advance to provide, how much to charge in discounts, whether a monthly minimum factoring volume or term of contract will be required, and other points of interest to the client. Therefore, it is important to make this information as accurate and thorough as possible. Leaving information fields blank will slow down your application review.

Knowing the prospect's **Business type** will help the factor determine which set up documents will be required, which are slightly different for corporations and LLC's than they are for partnerships and sole proprietors. The type of business doesn't matter to most factors (though many do not fund Sole Proprietors and require they incorporate or become an LLC prior to factoring); this information simply helps the factor prepare the correct documents.

The remaining information is needed for the factor to determine if the prospective business has any circumstances that might make a deal not doable. Factors must buy commercial receivables; that is, invoices from a business client to another business or government customer. They cannot deal with a private party who sells products or services. Thus the factor will require some kind of proof the client is a registered business. Documentation for this is usually a business license or registration of a DBA or trade name, or whatever the client's state may call such paperwork. An FEIN (**Federal Employer Identification Number**) is provided a registered business by the government. For Sole Proprietors, the owner's social security number is used as the FEIN number, but they must still have documentation showing their business is properly registered with the state, county, city, or other government body responsible for registering businesses in that location.

The Significance of UCCs

In order to understand why a factor asks about the existence of **UCC liens, delinquent taxes, litigation, judgments**, and **loans or lines of credit**, you must first understand what a UCC is. Let's take a moment to examine this.

UCC stands for Uniform Commercial Code, which is a branch of law that has to do with debts owed by one party to another. Any time one person or company provides money to another person or company, the one providing funds understandably wants assurances he will be paid back. The law makes provision for this in the Uniform Commercial Code.

Each Secretary of State's office in the country has a division that handles UCCs. When the party who provides money to another seeks greater security of repayment, the providing party will complete a UCC-1 form and is referred to as the "Secured Party." The person or company receiving the funds is called the "Debtor" on the UCC-1 form. When this form is completed and registered with the Secretary of State, a lien is put in place which secures the collateral of the secured party. The collateral is whatever the secured party says it is on the form; for factors, collateral is at least the client's accounts receivable, and often other or all assets of the company as well.

When this lien is filed, the information becomes a matter of public record. Think of it as a nationwide bulletin board, notifying everyone that the secured party has first rights to the collateral if there is ever a problem recovering the money. Why is this important?

When everything goes smoothly, a UCC filing is unnecessary. A borrower pays back her bank loan with regular payments, is never late, the bank gets its money back, and everybody is happy. Likewise, a factoring client's customers pay their invoices, the factor gets his money back, and everybody is happy. In such transactions a UCC filing has no significance.

However, such perfect transactions do not always occur in the real world. If a borrower defaults on a loan and declares bankruptcy, the bank stands to lose the remaining unpaid principal. If a factoring client has outstanding invoices that are uncollectible and the client's business declares bankruptcy, the factor stands to lose just like the bank. Having a UCC filed – and having it filed before anyone else – will provide some protection to these secured parties.

Let's use an example. When they started the factoring relationship, Factor A filed a UCC-1 form which secured the accounts receivable and assets of Client B. They factor for a period of time, when unfortunately Client B falls on difficult times and ends up with

$500,000 worth of debts he cannot repay. His assets are only $100,000. Sadly, Client B feels the only way out of the problem is to declare bankruptcy, which he does.

However, Factor A has purchased $250,000 worth of Client B's receivables. Most of these invoices are paid by the customers, but $75,000 is determined to be uncollectible and Client B is of course unable to pay them. Without a UCC filed, Factor A loses the $75,000.

However, Factor A filed the UCC and did so before any other secured party, thereby placing himself in "first position." When the bankruptcy is complete, the determination is made that there is a total of $100,000 in remaining assets in Client B's company, which must be distributed to its debtors. Being in first position, Factor A is first in line. He receives the $75,000 owed, and Lender C, who is in second position, is next in line to receive what she is owed. If Lender C is owed $50,000, she will only receive the remaining $25,000 in assets, and the rest must be written off as a loss. In this scenario, parties in third or lower positions are out of luck.

As you can see, debtors are paid back in the order of their UCC filing position, which is determined solely by filing date. The first to file is in first position. Bankruptcy disbursements are not made by simply determining the amount everyone is owed and splitting up the assets equally between them. The remaining goods go to those first in line (after the trustee and attorneys are paid, that is). If Client B's assets were determined to have been only $50,000, Factor A would have received $50,000 and lost the remaining $25,000. Lender C would have been completely left in the cold.

Therefore, as you can well understand, any factor or bank will want be in first position with every one of its clients. If a client wants to factor and already has a bank loan or line, the bank has no doubt filed a UCC already. If the bank can be persuaded to subordinate its position to a factor, the factor will likely accept this client. If a bank will not subordinate, the factor will be required to take a second position and will probably decline the deal. Wouldn't you?

Likewise, the presence of tax delinquencies, judgments, and the like are likely to involve liens which will put the parties involved in first position. Unless these situations can be worked out – and sometimes they can, particularly tax liens – the deal will probably not be doable for the factor. No first position usually means no deal.

The other information that is more typically required by larger factors – **annual sales, business financials, tax returns,** and so on – indicate a business is larger and able to meet the level of receivables and business sophistication these larger factors require.

As you can see, a relatively simple application form can enable a factor to determine quickly if a prospective client presents a desirable relationship for the factor. If she doesn't, the factor will decline and the client will need to look for a factor more suited to her business. If the problem is with customers who have poor or no credit standing, or the existence of liens or other problems which will severely jeopardize the factor's capital, the business may simply not be factorable.

Sometimes clients wonder why factors want so much information. Exchange places with the factor for a moment. If you were asked to provide significant cash to a total stranger who came to you seeking thousands of dollars – even tens or hundreds of thousands of dollars – what would you want to know about this stranger? Would you want to learn as much as possible about his business, customers, experience, personal character, and honesty?

Factors, who are in the position of providing significant amounts of money to prospective clients (who arrive as total strangers), understandably want to know these things. Again, providing the most thorough and accurate information is imperative.

Due Diligence Factors Perform

Once an application has been processed and the client is pre-approved, the factor will perform due diligence before granting final approval. The specific due diligence that is performed is up to each factor. Some factors will carry out all of the due diligence procedures described below; other factors will perform some of the procedures; still others may skip everything entirely. The decision is the factor's because the factor's money is on the line. Generally the larger the dollar amounts involved, the more thorough the underwriting will be.

Remember that obtaining this information costs the factor money. How much these costs total depends on the sources used to obtain the information and how much information is sought. The factor's cost to obtain this information is reflected in the due diligence fees he may charge.

Some clients are a bit wary of paying due diligence fees. They need to realize that factors are not in business to make money from due diligence fees: due diligence is simply a tool to minimize risk. No factor wants to collect due diligence fees and simply decline your account in order to pocket the fees. Due diligence charges cover their costs. Factors make their income from discounts charged for advancing money, and that doesn't happen until the invoices are paid. Therefore making sure the invoices *will be* paid is what due diligence is all about.

Here is a list of commonly run due diligence procedures, with a look at each one in detail

- Customer credit
- Public records searches
- Criminal records search of client
- Asset search of client

Customer Credit

This is the most common form of due diligence and can be obtained from a variety of sources. Most often factors have accounts with major credit reporting agencies such as Dun & Bradstreet, Experian, Trans Union, or many others. Reports from these agencies vary widely in scope, information included, and price. A single credit report can range in price from about $5 for a very simple report with quite limited information, to well over $100 for extremely thorough data. Adequate information for most factors will usually range in cost from about $5 to $30 per report. If you have a long list of customers whose credit a factor needs to check, you can see how his cost will add up quickly. Accurate aging reports you provide may help tremendously here, but most factors still want information supplied by a professional credit reporting agency, which includes some kind of credit rating in the form of a numeric and/or letter score.

Many of these credit agencies offer updates on companies whose credit has previously been checked. This service keeps the factor informed of any changes to a company's credit standing, which in turn is very valuable information for you. If your customer's credit rating suddenly takes a nose dive, you may want to change the terms you offer to protect yourself from unexpectedly slow payments or even bad debt, or simply stop selling to that customer altogether.

Public Records Searches

Searches of public records are typically performed on both a prospective client and her customers. The searches look for **UCC filings, tax liens, civil judgments,** and **bankruptcies**. While this information is usually included in credit reports mentioned above, factors often use other sources for this information in case a credit report has missed something...which happens.

A **UCC** search informs the factor if a prospective client has any UCC liens in place, the importance of which has been described earlier. If a UCC filing is found, the factor will need to determine if it is still in place and if so, if the filer will terminate or subordinate. UCC filings on a client's customers are of little significance to a factor because he will file a UCC only on his clients, not their customers.

Tax liens and **civil judgments** include dollar amounts and show filing dates. If these obligations have been released, the amount that was owed and paid, and the date of the release, is stated. You know if a tax lien is in place against you or your business, and non-disclosure of this information will bring your honesty into question. Therefore, be sure to provide full disclosure on the application form. Presenting this information will not necessarily kill your chances of being accepted; *not* doing so can very well kill the deal, even if your customer base is strong. If you are less than honest in your application, a factor will be even more doubtful of your integrity once money begins to change hands. No factor wants to do business with a dishonest individual. Do you?

Tax liens found on your customers' records may or may not be worthy of note. If the amount is fairly small, it will probably not impact their business. However, if a small or moderate sized company has a significant tax problem, chances are their financial position is not strong and they may not able to pay in a way you desire. Knowing this before extending terms can save you a lot of money and headaches.

Civil judgments against you or your customer may indicate a problem if the number of judgments is large or the dollar amount high. Because the effort one spends to attain a judgment can be extensive, the fact that these show up on one's record bears some weight.

For example, say a relatively small business has ten judgments that have been filed in the last five years. Each judgment is for $2,500 or more. That means on average, twice each year for five consecutive years, a situation has arisen in which another party has been awarded at least $2,500 by a court. For a company that does $100,000 a year in sales – less than $10,000 a month – this is a significant blot on its record. One wonders how many other people have been burned by this company but not bothered to seek a judgment. If you were a factor, would you want to buy their receivables?

However, suppose your customer is a multi-billion dollar corporation with hundreds of offices around the world. This company owns dozens of subsidiaries and has tens of thousands of employees. A search turns up ten civil judgments which also average $2,500. In this situation, these judgments are probably insignificant for such a huge company. One doubts they indicate the customer will be unlikely or unable to pay factored invoices. That is, after all, what a factor wants to know.

Criminal Records Search

If a business owner has a record of fraud or other criminal activity, factors will be understandably reluctant to advance him cash. While fraud is a rare occurrence, most factors are not unfamiliar with people who have attempted (or succeeded in) ripping them off. As a result there are "fraud boards" provided by various web sites which alert factors of dishonest clients who sometimes go from one factor to another in search of a new victim. Factors who are in competition with each other are also quick to let one another know when a scam has been attempted, or when they simply have suspicions. What's more, running criminal background checks is a common due diligence task, especially when significant funds are involved.

Asset Search

Locating assets of a prospective client can be done easily with the right software or internet services. Some factors will want to know a prospective client's net worth to see if the amount could cover potential losses should problems develop.

If you possess few or no assets or your credit is poor, rest assured factors are neither surprised nor put off to find this. Few assets, poor credit, and a bankruptcy in your past will not mean a factor will turn you away (unlike bank applicants). However, having some assets that would help the factor recover her funds if a severe problem ever developed can make her feel more comfortable purchasing your receivables in the first place. Again, having as full a picture of your business and financial circumstances as possible will enable a factor to know how best to help you with the services and capital at her disposal.

Closing Documents

Once a factor's due diligence is complete there is one last step before receiving your first funding. Closing documents which spell out all the particulars of your business relationship with the factor need to be signed.

Again, not every factor will utilize every document mentioned below, but most will use many of them. They are provided here so you understand what these documents are and the purpose they serve. In some cases, the documents listed will be combined with other documents. For example, a limited power of attorney is often contained within the contract. These documents may also be called different names, but the essential information is similar.

Factoring Checklist

This is a handy form which lists the documents needed to open a factoring account, and allows you or the factor to simply check off needed items as they are obtained.

Term Sheet

This sheet summarizes all the terms of the factoring relationship. These include the initial credit line, advance percentage, factoring discounts, other fees such as bank wires or overnight charges, recourse terms, reserve terms, minimum invoice charges, minimum monthly charges if any, term length of contract if any, and probably a date after which the stated terms expire if not signed by both parties.

Contract (A/R Purchase Agreement)

This is the heart of the agreement between the factor and client, and often includes some of the documents below. Since it is written in legal language be sure you understand everything this document contains. Many business owners have their attorneys review this and the other documents prior to signing.

Limited Power of Attorney

This document allows the factor to carry out certain activities in order to service your account. This may include opening mail addressed to you at the factor's address, endorsing checks paying factored invoices if they are made in your company's name, depositing these checks in the factor's bank account, contacting your customers and perhaps negotiating on your behalf the payment of your invoices, and the like. This power of attorney is an important part of the factoring relationship and is commonly included in closing documents.

Discount Schedule

This document spells out specifically how your factoring discount is calculated. Be sure this is clear and you understand what this says, so you don't later think you are being overcharged.

Personal Guarantee

This document is used to put the factor in a more secure position if your account runs into trouble. A personal guarantee states that if your business is unable to repay any money owed the factor, the guarantor/s will pay the factor from his/her/their personal assets. Many factors require this document, some do not. If the business is located or incorporated in a community property state, the spouse of the guarantor may have to sign this document as well.

IRS Form 8821

This document is used by the factor to secure his collateral, which might be jeopardized if IRS decides to slap you with a tax lien. By the factor's filing this form (which you must sign), you are allowing IRS to notify the factor of any impending action against you.

Because the factor's money is tied up in your receivables and IRS will likely garnish these receivables, the factor understandably wants to be informed before this happens. Form 8821 allows for this notification, and in fact enables the factor to help you work out of a tax problem by making sure IRS is paid from future factored transactions.

Proof of Business Registration

Because a factor works with businesses as opposed to private parties, proof of your business registration needs to be demonstrated. The first page of your **Articles of Incorporation**, if you are incorporated, provides this. So will the first page of an LLC Agreement. You need not provide the full document of the Articles or Agreement, as these can be quite lengthy; the factor merely wants documented proof these exist.

Partnerships will need to provide the **Partnership Agreement**. Sole Proprietors will need proof of their business registration which is called various names in different states or regions. These names include **Business License, DBA Registration, Fictitious Name Filing**, and the like. Ordinarily a copy of this document, which the state or other government entity provided when you registered your business, is requested. If you have never formally registered your business and have been operating as a private party, you will need to obtain proper business registration in order to factor your receivables.

Corporate Resolution

If your business is a corporation, this document needs to be signed by your board of directors. It states they have formally granted you permission to sign the closing documents and use the factor's services.

Personal ID of Principal/s

In order to run due diligence checks on your company's principals and/or those responsible for the funds your factor will provide, many factors will require a driver's license, social security number, or other personal identification.

Notice of Assignment

This is a letter that informs your customers of the factoring relationship, and instructs the customer to remit payment to your new remittance address. The factor will provide the wording needed and usually all you need to do is sign the letter. You or the factor will then put it in your customer's hands so payments will be handled properly. This is explained more fully in the next chapter, "Telling Your Customers."

11

Telling Your Customers

What Will My Customers Think?

A common concern among many business owners who consider factoring their receivables is their customers' reaction. They might worry, "Will they think I'm in financial trouble?" "Will they stop doing business with me?" "Will they refuse to pay a factor?" While these concerns are not uncommon, the vast majority of the time they are quite groundless, as is soon discovered.

If you sell to very large corporations, chances are quite good they have other vendors who are also factoring receivables to this customer. If this business requires 30 day terms and/or pays even later than that, you can be sure this squeezes other vendors just like it squeezes you. In fact, you may be surprised to find how common factoring is with large corporations; some even have separate divisions within their A/P department for factored accounts.

If you sell to smaller businesses, you can inform them that because you have obtained financing, your business is now in a stronger position and can serve them even better than before. Your confidence will dispel any hint of doubt in your customer's mind. That confidence springs from the immediate cash that will soon be in your hands once your invoices have been factored.

Most factors provide a Notice of Assignment (mentioned earlier) to give your customers. This notice simply makes the transition to factoring smoother for everyone. If a customer questions what this means, you can simply and honestly tell him you are outsourcing your receivables management, just like many companies outsource their payroll management. Doing so is giving you improved cash flow and frees you from a time-consuming task that is not profitable for your business. By outsourcing this job, you're now able to provide an even better product or service.

Not only will most people see the wisdom and be agreeable to this new arrangement, some will want to know how they can get this service for their business. When this happens, you may be able to earn a referral fee just for giving the factor a name and phone number (with that person's permission, of course). Client referrals like this are quite common and an excellent means for factors to gain new business.

You will need your customer's cooperation which means verifying with the factor your invoice is valid and approved for payment. By signing and returning the Notice of Assignment (if required by your factor), your customer is stating he is aware of the assignment of your invoices and will make future payments to your new remittance address (the factor's). You can help the factor by making sure the proper person in your customer's business receives, signs and returns the Notice, and the bookkeeper or payables department makes the address or bank account change.

Only in very rare instances may you run across a customer who will not cooperate. The number of such individuals is extremely small, and uncooperative customers are far fewer than most people first imagine. Customers who are good business owners appreciate the need for cash to run a company. Therefore if a customer resists working with your factor, you have likely experienced other issues with this customer and may already consider him less than ideal.

Factors often report payment histories to credit reporting agencies (where do you think that information comes from?!), and slow-paying customers who are aware of this don't want their poor payment patterns reported. Alternately, when slow paying customers learn you are factoring, they may be inclined to pay you more promptly because they know the factor will report their pattern. This is especially true with large corporate customers who want to maintain their good credit rating.

Notification Versus Non-notification

Factoring with notification to your customers is the standard practice and works just fine for nearly all factoring clients. Factors will prefer to work this way because invoices can be verified easily and nothing needs to be handled secretively.

However, on occasion a client will insist on a non-notification factoring basis. This may mean your factor never contacts your customers to verify invoices or check on slow payment. Alternately, the factor's account executive will contact a customer and state she is "Jane Smith of ABC Widget Company," rather than "Jane Smith of First Financial Services," in order to keep the factoring relationship transparent to the customer. Either way, more risk and/or more work are involved for the factor and you should expect to pay extra for this service. Therefore be sure your business or customers absolutely require this arrangement or you will be paying more than you need to. Remember, the vast majority of factoring is done on a notification basis.

12
Factoring Procedures

An earlier flowchart summarized the steps involved prior to funding. Once your account is set up those steps do not need to be done again; you simply submit more invoices each time funding is needed. This quick submittal process is one of the biggest advantages of factoring: you usually obtain cash for your receivables in just a day or two – and sometimes even the same day. You don't have to wait weeks or even months, as with traditional financing, to have your cash in hand.

On the next page is a flowchart that shows this recurring transaction.

Factoring Transaction Flowchart

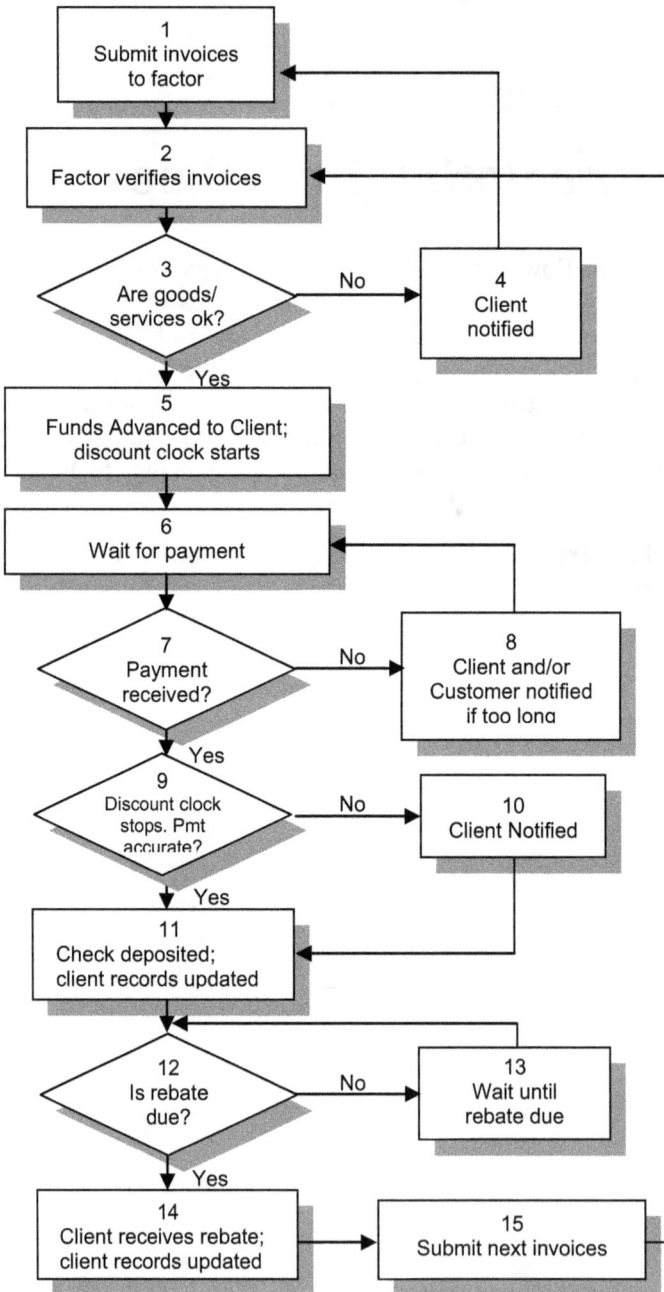

```
┌─────────────────────┐
│          1          │
│   Submit invoices   │◄──────────────────┐
│     to factor       │                   │
└─────────────────────┘                   │
          │                               │
          ▼                               │
┌─────────────────────┐                   │
│          2          │◄──────────────┐   │
│ Factor verifies     │               │   │
│ invoices            │               │   │
└─────────────────────┘               │   │
          │                           │   │
          ▼                           │   │
        ╱ 3 ╲          No    ┌──────────────┐
       ╱ Are  ╲─────────────►│      4       │
       ╲ goods/╱              │   Client     │
        ╲ services ok?        │  notified    │
          │ Yes               └──────────────┘
          ▼
┌─────────────────────┐
│          5          │
│ Funds Advanced to   │
│ Client; discount    │
│ clock starts        │
└─────────────────────┘
          │
          ▼
┌─────────────────────┐
│          6          │◄──────────────┐
│   Wait for payment  │               │
└─────────────────────┘               │
          │                           │
          ▼                           │
        ╱ 7 ╲          No    ┌──────────────┐
       ╱Payment╲────────────►│      8       │
       ╲received?╱            │ Client and/or│
          │ Yes               │ Customer     │
          ▼                   │ notified if  │
        ╱ 9 ╲          No     │ too long     │
       ╱Discount╲             └──────────────┘
       ╲ clock   ╱     No    ┌──────────────┐
        ╲stops. Pmt─────────►│     10       │
          accurate?          │Client Notified│
          │ Yes               └──────────────┘
          ▼
┌─────────────────────┐
│         11          │
│ Check deposited;    │◄──────────────┐
│ client records      │               │
│ updated             │               │
└─────────────────────┘               │
          │                           │
          ▼                           │
        ╱ 12 ╲         No    ┌──────────────┐
       ╱Is rebate╲──────────►│     13       │
       ╲  due?    ╱          │  Wait until  │
          │ Yes               │ rebate due   │
          ▼                   └──────────────┘
┌─────────────────────┐     ┌──────────────┐
│         14          │     │     15       │
│ Client receives     │────►│ Submit next  │
│ rebate; client      │     │ invoices     │
│ records updated     │     └──────────────┘
└─────────────────────┘
```

Invoice Submission

The first step to obtaining cash for your receivables is to submit one or more invoices to your factor. This is done with a Schedule of Accounts, also referred to as an Assignment Sheet, Assignment Schedule, or other names. The Schedule of Accounts is simply a form on which you list the invoices you're factoring, and include the customer's company name, the invoice number/s to that customer, the invoice date, perhaps a P.O. or other reference number, and the invoice amount.

Filling a Schedule properly is important because it is an extension of your contract with the factor, and the means by which you legally assign the receivables. Therefore you must be sure to sign each and every Schedule or the assignment isn't complete and the factor will not advance funds. The total of the invoices and advance to be made are calculated on this form, and once it is received the factor can proceed with your advance.

Factors vary in their preferences as to how invoices are submitted. Some will require you provide original invoices, backup paperwork, and copies of both for their file. The factor then mails or faxes the invoices to your customers. This assures there will be no confusion or duplication of an invoice sent to your customer. Many factors will also stamp the invoice with verbiage indicating it has been assigned to the factor, which provides added protection in case payment is sent to you.

Some factors will actually create your invoices for you once you have provided necessary information. Most factors who provide this service will charge a fee for this extra work, and if billing is a task you'd like to outsource or the factor can do it more cost effectively than your current practice, this can be an added benefit of factoring. Indeed, some factoring companies simply become the A/R department of their clients.

Some do this by using software which enables you, the client, to submit your invoice information online. The software then generates the invoice and the factor emails, faxes, or prints and mails the invoice to your customer, saving you the time and expense of doing so.

Some factors will prefer to have you fax or email your invoices and backup paperwork to them along with your signed Schedule. You are then responsible for mailing or faxing the original invoices to your customers. Not all factors allow this, however, as there is greater margin for error.

Customer Verification

The next step for the factor is to be sure the invoices on a Schedule are accurate and acceptable to your customers who will be paying the bills. This is done by verifying the invoices, which can be done in a number of ways.

Most factors prefer to have an authorized signature from your customer which indicates the amount on the invoice is correct, the product or service has been received and is acceptable, and the customer will pay the invoice to the remit-to address of the factor. You may provide a place for this signature at the bottom of your invoice or on a separate document agreeable to each party.

By signing this document the signatory is committing your customer's company to payment, so be sure the person is not only authorized to sign, but knowledgeable as to the receipt and acceptability of the goods or service rendered. If a signature is received and the customer later claims there was something wrong, an unnecessary problem has occurred.

The purpose of verifications is to avoid such problems. In fact invoice verifications often act as a quality control device for you. If your customer has as issue or dispute over an invoice, this can come to light during verification. Thus you solve the problem immediately, keep your customer happy, and obtain immediate cash at the same time.

Written verifications take various shapes according to your industry. For example, staffing agencies can usually use time cards signed by their customers as verification that the invoices corresponding to the time cards are approved. Likewise, a signed bill of lading, receiving slip, or work order may also work fine. Just be sure you, the factor, and your customer all are on the same page with regard to the significance of these signed documents.

If a signature cannot be obtained factors will frequently verify invoices with a phone call. Typically you will supply your account executive with the name and phone number of the person who will provide verification. The account executive will phone this person, ask if the product or service has been received in proper condition, receive assurances that customer is satisfied with the transaction, and that the bill will be paid to the factor's address. The account executive will typically make note of the person providing verification and date of the call.

This usually takes no more than a minute or two, provides the factor with the assurance the transaction should flow smoothly, and provides you with the knowledge that there should be no problems after you receive your advance.

Your First Funding

When you are new to factoring your first funding will be the slowest because necessary tasks need to be performed for the first (and often only) time. First the factor will need to complete his due diligence to establish your account. Then you will need to determine which customers you wish to factor. Finally the factor will determine which customers are acceptable to him and which invoices will be funded to begin.

Some factors will accept only "fresh" invoices for your first funding – that is, invoices which have not yet been submitted to your customers. This is simply to avoid factoring invoices which are already in your customer's systems for payment, or perhaps have already paid and are on their way to you. Other factors may purchase "seasoned" invoices – invoices already submitted to your customers – as long as they haven't been outstanding too long. In general, it's best to start with fresh invoices if you can.

Other items which make your first funding take longer include the determination of the methods of verifying your invoices, then performing the verifications. Once these procedures are in place and everyone is accustomed to the verification process, whatever it may be, future advances happen quickly.

129

Future Advances

Once you've submitted a couple Schedules and the first few payments are received by the factor, your transactions should be smooth, consistent, and reliable. You'll simply submit your signed Schedule and invoices, the factor receives them and obtains necessary verifications, and then provides your advance. Usually the only hold up to receiving your cash is caused by some problem obtaining a verification. Therefore the more you can help with this, the faster you receive your advance.

The means by which your advance is provided will depend on your factor's practices and your own convenience. If you live or work near your factor's office, you may prefer to go to the factor's office to pick up your advance and rebate checks. Many factors prefer to make electronic ACH payments to your bank account.

If you are not located near the factor, he may use a bank wire or overnight a check to you. These methods usually involve an added charge so be sure you understand what these will cost if they are necessary. Bank wires usually involve two charges: one to send a wire (factor's cost passed on to you) and another to receive it (your cost charged by your bank).

Payments

Most factors require payments from your customers be sent to the factor's address. The reasons for this should be apparent as both the factor's interest (more security) and your interest (the discount clock stops sooner) are served by this procedure. Having payments sent to the factor assures the factor that the check will not be inadvertently deposited in your bank account. This can happen quite innocently and is not an uncommon occurrence.

Here's a typical scenario: your administrative assistant picks up the mail, finds checks there and deposits them in the bank on the way back to the office – not realizing that one or some of those checks were factored payments. If you or your bookkeeper don't realize this has happened, that extra cash can easily be spent over the course of daily business and by the time you catch the error, repaying the factor can be difficult if your cash flow is especially tight. What's more, because the factor has not received payment, your discount clock continues to tick and you end up paying more in discounts than you should have.

Worse, if depositing factored checks – or "converting" them in factoring parlance – is done intentionally, you have willfully committed criminal fraud and are exposing yourself to some very serious consequences. This has been covered in the chapter "Faulty Assumptions and Mistakes to Avoid." You must ***never*** do this, regardless of how badly you need the cash.

Rebates

When your customer pays an invoice in full, the factor first reimburses herself for the advance, keeps the discount earned, then owes you a rebate for the balance. How your rebate is paid will vary from one factor to the next so you want to clearly understand your factor's procedure. If your margins are slim, your rebate may be a large portion of your profit, making it even more important.

You benefit most when a factor pays your rebate as soon as possible after receiving your customer's payment. However, in order to minimize their own processing time and therefore overhead, many factors pay rebates once a month for the previous month's accumulated rebates due. Others, although not very many, pay all the rebates from a Schedule once all the invoices on that Schedule have been paid. This provides a reserve against short payments or non-payments from your customers.

Other factors pay rebates on a per invoice basis, perhaps on a weekly or even daily basis. Factors who do this may withhold a portion of your rebate and place it in a reserve account, and build up that reserve until a certain threshold is reached. This might be calculated as a percentage of your credit limit with the factor, or a percentage of your outstanding invoices. In either case this reserve provides a hedge against short payments and non-payments and can come in very handy when a customer doesn't pay in full. Subtracting amounts owed from this reserve due to short payments means such deductions will not come from future advances, which can hurt your cash flow. Therefore creating such a reserve is actually a very prudent move and protects both you and the factor if your customer doesn't pay as expected. Such reserves may also or instead be accumulated from small deductions from your first advances when you start factoring. Again, ask your factor what her practice is.

Be sure your factor thoroughly explains her rebate and reserve procedures, that you understand these transactions completely, and that what was described is in fact what is practiced when rebates are due.

Conclusion

This book is written to enable you to determine if factoring will benefit your business, understand how factoring transactions take place, and envision the transformations factoring can make to your business. You've learned how to find a factor, what to ask, how to recognize a factor who is a good match for your business, and what you need to do to begin. The next step is up to you.

Taking the Next Step

If you've determined that factoring will benefit your business, the next step is to jot down the actions you need to take to get started. By writing them below you will be laying the groundwork to begin factoring your receivables to improve your cash flow.

Action Items

1. _____

2. _____

3. _____

4. _____

5. _____

6. _____

7. _____

8. _____

9. _____

10. _____

If this book was given to you by a factor or broker, you are well on your way to towards receiving **unlimited funds without a loan.** If you obtained this book on your own and are ready to find a factor, you have the information you need to begin the search. Finding or recognizing the right factor is now just a matter of applying what you've learned. The cash won't be far behind.

My sincere hope is that your business can benefit from factoring, become stronger and grow, and improve your life and the lives of those your business touches. Best wishes as you begin **Factoring: Sell Your Invoices Today, Get Cash Tomorrow!**

Glossary

Terms in the Definition column that are in bold print are included in this Glossary.

Term	Definition
Accounts Payable	Amounts owed to other companies for goods and services.
Accounts Receivable	Amounts owed by other companies for goods and services.
Advance	A percentage of an **Invoice** paid to a **Client** by a **Factor** upon sale of the invoice by the client to the factor.
ACH	Stands for "Automated Clearing House," a means of electronically transferring funds from one bank account to another.
Aging Report	A summary of a client's **Accounts Receivable**, broken down by customer and/or length of time the receivables have been outstanding.
Assets	Anything of commercial or exchange value a business, institution or individual owns. Assets include cash, property, and **Accounts Receivable**.
Assignment	Term used when **Accounts Receivable** are factored. The **Client**'s right to the accounts is sold, or assigned, to a Factor.
Bad Debt	Unpaid receivables which have been written off as uncollectable.
Balance Sheet	A financial report which lists a company's **Assets**, **Liabilities**, and the difference (shown as equity), on a given date.
Bank Wire	A means of electronically sending money from one bank account to another.

Broker	An individual or business who, for a fee, matches a company seeking factoring services with a **Factor** appropriate for that company's needs.
Cash Flow	The difference between cash received and cash paid out.
Client	A company who factors its **Accounts Receivable**
Credit-Reports	A report obtained from a commercial credit agency which lists the payment history, debts, public records, and credit risk of a company or individual.
Customer	The company who has received products or services from a **Client** and will pay the resulting **Invoice**(s). Referred to by some factors as the **Debtor**.
DBA	Abbreviation of "Doing Business As."
Debtor	The company who has received products or services from a **Client** and will pay the resulting **Invoice**(s). Referred to by some factors as the **Customer**.
Discount	The amount paid by the **Client** to the **Factor** for the factor's services; it is calculated by subtracting the total amount **Advance**d and **Rebate**d by the **Factor** from the face value of the **Invoice**.
Discount - Schedule	A document that shows the **Discount** paid to the **Factor** based on the length of time a **Customer** takes to pay an **Invoice**.
Due - Diligence	Information gathered by a **Factor** to determine whether or not to accept a **Client** and/or **Customer**. Also referred to as **Underwriting**.
Factor	A company or individual who purchases **Accounts Receivable** from a **Client** at a **Discount** from the face value of the **Receivables**.
Factoring	The sale of **Accounts Receivable** at a **Discount** to a **Factor**.
Fees	Amounts charged by a **Factor** for: a) **Application** and **Due Diligence** processing and/or b) funds transfer costs such as **Bank Wires** and overnight delivery.

Financial Statements	Reports which may be requested or required as part of a **Factor**'s **Due Diligence**. The most commonly requested are a **Income Statement** (also called a **Profit & Loss Statement**), a **Balance Sheet** and a business owner's personal **Net Worth Statement**
Fixed Costs	Expenses which do not vary with the volume of one's business.
Income Statement	A **Financial Statement** (sometimes called a Profit and Loss Statement) that shows the income, expenses, and net profit or net loss for a given period of time (usually monthly, quarterly, and yearly).
Invoice	A document from a company to a **Customer** that states the amount owed by a **Customer** for goods or services rendered by the company.
Liabilities	Claims on the **Assets** of a company or individual, excluding the owner's equity. Liabilities include **Accounts Payable**, other debts, taxes owed, etc
Limit	The maximum amount that will be **Ad-vanced** by a **Factor** to a **Client** for all **Customers** or for a specific **Customer**
Lien	A legal claim against property or other assets, submitted to state and/or county authorities. **Factors** commonly file a **Lien (UCC-1)** against a **Client**'s **Assets** to secure against possible loss.
Loan	A sum of money provided to an individual or company that is to be repaid with interest. **Factoring** is not a Loan.
Net Worth Statement	The list of an individual's **Assets**, **Liabilities**, and the difference between them.
Non-notification	Term used when a **Customer** is intentionally not made aware that a **Client** is **Factoring** their **Invoices**

Non-recourse Factoring	If a **Customer** does not pay the **Factor** within a specific period of time, the **Client** is not responsible for repaying the **Factor** the **Advance** and **Discount** (provided the invoice is not disputed).
Notice of Assignment	A document given to a **Customer** stating a **Client**'s invoices have been factored and that payment should be made to the **Factor**.
Notification	The term used when a **Customer** is made aware that a **Client** is **Factoring**
Overhead	The costs of a business that do not include cost of goods sold; sometimes called indirect costs and expenses.
Personal Guaranty	A contractual agreement between a **Factor** and business owner or corporation executive in which the owner or executive assumes personal responsibility and liability for the obligations of the business to the **Factor**.
Purchase Order	A document itemizing an order for goods or services from a **Customer** that includes items desired and prices.
Purchase Order Funding	A means of financing by which a **Factor** or other funding source **Advances** cash for a **Purchase Order**.
Quantity Discounts	A price reduction received by companies when they purchase larger amounts of a product.
Rebate	The balance of the amount paid for an **Invoice** minus the **Advance** plus **Discount**, which is paid by a **Factor** to a **Client** after receiving payment from a **Customer**. Its formula: Rebate = Invoice Amount Paid − (Advance + Discount).
Recourse Factoring	If a **Customer** does not pay the **Factor** within a specific period of time, the **Client** is responsible for repaying the **Factor** the **Advance** and **Discount**.
Reserve	The **Invoice** amount minus the **Advance** plus the **Discount**, which a **Factor** holds until a **Rebate** is due. Other reserves may be held as well

Schedule of Accounts	A document provided by a **Factor** that lists all **Invoices** factored at a given time by a **Client**. It includes at least the **Customer, Invoice** number, **Invoice** amount, **Invoice** date, and signature of the **Client** with a declaration of **Assignment** to the **Factor**.
Spot - Factoring	The process of **Factoring** one or very few invoices on a one-time or rare basis
UCC-1	Abbreviated term for **Uniform Commercial Code**. A document filed with the Secretary of State and/or County Recording Clerk in which the Client's property being secured is located. With factoring, this filing evidences and perfects a factor's security interest in a **Client**'s personal property, especially **Accounts Receivable**.
UCC- 3	Abbreviated term for **Uniform Commercial Code**. A document filed with the Secretary of State and/or County Recording Clerk to declare a change in a **UCC-1** previously filed, such as termination of security interest or another change.
Underwriting	Information gathered by a **Factor** to determine whether or not to accept a **Client** and/or **Customer**. Also referred to as **Due Diligence.**
Uniform Commercial Code	A law which regulates the transfer of personal property.
Variable Costs	Expenses which vary with the volume of business.
Venture Capital	Funds invested in a business usually considered high-risk, which commonly results in the investors owning a portion of the business. Expenses which vary with the volume of business.

Verification   The procedure by which a **Factor** confirms the validity of **Assigned Invoices** from a **Client**. Ordinarily, a **Factor** will determine the product has been rendered to the satisfaction of the **Customer**, the **Customer** intends to pay, and payment will be made to the Factor.

Volume,   The total amount of **Invoices** factored by a **Client** during
Monthly   a month's time.

"Top 10" Ebooks for Business Owners:

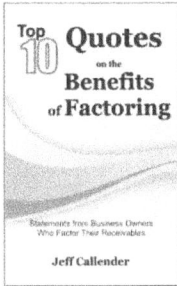

Top 10 Quotes on the Benefits of Factoring

Statements from Business Owners
Who Factor Their Receivables

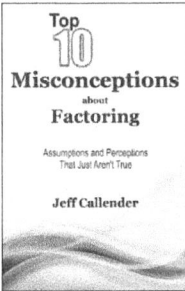

Top 10 Misconceptions about Factoring

Assumptions and Perceptions
That Just Aren't True

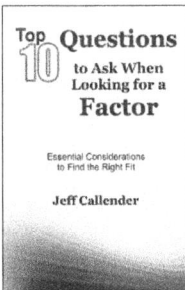

Top 10 Questions to Ask When Looking for a Factor

Essential Considerations
to Find the Right Fit

The above ebooks are available in the following formats from DashPointPublishing.com:

- PDF
- Kindle
- iPad & Android

Acknowledgments

I would like to thank the following people for the important parts they played in creating this book:

The many clients I've worked with over the years who have shown me not only the value of factoring to business owners, but the importance of providing top caliber service no matter what type of business one has.

Nicole Jones for her proofreading skills and creating the ebook versions of books of all my titles, and making them available to the world.

Anne Gordon for her proofreading skills and valuable experience, insights and comments.

Cover image credit: © ragsac/123RF.com

Important Notice

Also by Jeff Callender

Paperbacks and Ebooks

The Small Factor Series includes 5 titles:

1. *Factoring Wisdom: A Preview of Buying Receivables*
   Short Sayings and Straight Talk for New & Small Factors © 2012

2. *Fundamentals for Factors*
   How You Can Make Large Returns in Small Receivables © 2012

3. *How to Run a Small Factoring Business*
   Make Money in Little Deals the Big Guys Brush Off © 2012

4. *Factoring Case Studies*
   Essential Lessons from 30 Real Factoring Clients
   1st edition ©2003, 2005; 2nd edition © 2012

5. *Marketing Methods for Small Factors & Brokers*
   Tools from the Trenches to Make Your Factoring Business Thrive!© 2012
   Factoring: Sell Your Invoices Today, Get Cash Tomorrow
   How to Obtain Unlimited Funds without a Loan © 2012

eBooks

For Factoring Clients:

Accounting Methods for Factors & Their Clients	© 2012
Top 10 Quotes on the Benefits of Factoring	© 2012
Top 10 Misconceptions about Factoring	© 2012
Top 10 Questions to Ask When Looking for a Factor	© 2012

For Factors:

Accounting Methods for Factors & Their Clients	© 2012
How I Run My One-Person Factoring Business	© 2008, 2012
How I Run My Virtual Factoring Office	© 2012
Top 10 Insights about Factoring Prospects	© 2008, 2012
Top 10 Illusions about Risk and Loss	© 2008, 2012
Top 10 Statements You Never Want to Hear	© 2008, 2012
10 Key Points to Look for in Factoring Software	© 2008, 2012

Spreadsheet Calculators

APR and Income Calculators © 2002, 2012

Software

FactorFox Software © 2006 – current year

Websites

www.DashPointPublishing.com www.SmallFactor.com
www.DashPointFinancial.com www.SmallFactorAcademy.com
www.FactorFox.com www.FactorFind.com

About the Author

Jeff Callender had an unusual start to his business career. Though he is the son and grandson of businessmen, he began his working life as a pastor.

After earning a college degree in Sociology and a Master of Divinity degree, he served three churches in Washington state over 14 years. While he found ministry rewarding, he realized he had an entrepreneurial spirit which gradually pulled him toward business.

He left his career in the church and about a year later stumbled onto factoring. He began as a broker but after numerous referrals were declined only because of their small size, he started factoring very small clients himself. His career as a factor – and as a pioneer in the niche of very small receivables factoring – was thus born in 1994.

He has worked with a great number of very small business owners in need of factoring. He wrote his first book, *Factoring Small Receivables*, in 1995, and since then has written numerous books, ebooks, and articles, and spoken at many events in the factoring industry. His writing and two decades of experience have established him as a leading authority in the niche of small business factoring.

Jeff is the President of three companies he started. Dash Point Financial provides factoring services to small business owners throughout the U.S. It also provides the nucleus of his experience for writing. Learn more at DashPointFinancial.com.

Dash Point Publishing publishes and sells his books and ebooks, as well as those of other authors who write about factoring. His paperbacks are available from DashPointPublishing.com, as well as

Amazon, the Kindle bookstore, Apple's iBookstore, and other online ebook sellers. Dash Point Publishing's website provides additional materials such as legal documents for smaller factoring companies.

FactorFox Software offers a cloud-based database solution for factors to track their client transactions. Originally based on his own company's back-office operational needs, readers of his books will feel right at home using the software in their own factoring companies. It has become one of the top platforms for the industry and is used by factoring companies throughout the world. More information can be found at FactorFox.com.

Having grown up in southern California, Jeff now lives in Tacoma, Washington with his wife, dog, and two cats. He has a grown son and daughter.

www.ingramcontent.com/pod-product-compliance
Lightning Source LLC
Chambersburg PA
CBHW060608200326
41521CB00007B/699